League of Nations

Diplomacy

fine in dj ug lt

Matt soil:

on net to one numbers

THE SENATE AND THE VERSAILLES MANDATE SYSTEM

BY

RAYFORD W. LOGAN
Howard University

The Minorities Publishers
Washington, D. C.
1945

TO 750,000,000 DEPENDENT PEOPLE

PREFACE

Striking similarities between the mandate system established by the Treaty of Versailles and the trusteeship plan adopted at the San Francisco Conference make timely an analysis of the attitude of the Senate toward the World War I mandates. Even Denna F. Fleming in *The United States and the League of Nations, 1918-1920* (1932), still the best book on that subject, devoted very little space to the mandates. This study not only covers in detail the debates on the mandates, but it develops the subject as a connected theme and it also offers some new interpretations and observations. Despite the continuity of the theme, it is not presented *in vacuo* but is made an integral part of the crucial debates that resulted in the rejection of the Treaty of Versailles.

Armenia, the only mandate that the United States was asked to accept, received most of the sympathy largely because of the "atrocities" inflicted upon a Christian population by the "unspeakable Turk." But not even this appeal was sufficient to overcome the basic determination of the Senate to keep the United States out of the League of Nations. Only one senator showed any apparently real interest in the former German colonies in Africa, and his reservation in favor of acceptance of a mandate over them received three votes. There was a glimmer of realization of the future strategic importance of the Pacific mandates. Now that these have been conquered at the cost of tremendous and heroic sacrifice and their strategic importance is generally recognized, the attitude of the Senate toward them may well be decidedly different from what it was toward mandates in general at the end of World War I. It should be exceedingly interesting to note whether the constitutional and financial objections and the unwillingness to send American "boys" to die in their defense will have equal weight in the Senate debates on the San Francisco trusteeship plan.

These chapters are part of a larger work soon to be published on "The African Mandates in World Politics." I wish to express my most sincere thanks to the Rosenwald Fund for a fellowship that enabled me to use my sabbatical year for the gathering of material upon which this and the forthcoming book are based.

RAYFORD WHITTINGHAM LOGAN.

Howard University
Washington, D. C.
June 23, 1945.

CONTENTS

Chapter I

INTRODUCTION

Quarrels over the disposition of the colonial spoils of war provoked some of the most bitterly-contested crises of the Paris peace negotiations in 1919. Woodrow Wilson wished to reduce the area of international conflict by placing these spoils under some international authority that would also protect and promote the welfare of the Native inhabitants. Missionary organizations and liberal parties, especially in England, had placed the humanitarian aspects of the problem above the international issues involved. But three of the British dominions—the Union of South Africa, Australia, and New Zealand—emerged from the war greedy with imperialistic desires. Britain, France, Italy and Japan had signed secret treaties during the war for the distribution of some of the enemy possessions.[1] The compromise inevitably resulting from this clash of humanitarianism and imperialism was embodied in article 22 of the Covenant of the League of Nations.[2]

Under this compromise, as frequently happens, the imperialists got most of the substance while the humanitarians got the verbal shadow. The individual nations that became mandatories on behalf of the League were given the actual administration of the mandated areas under the supervision of the Council. They were to make annual reports to a permanent commission showing the extent to which they had carried out the provisions of article 22 which proclaimed the principle that the well-being and development of "peoples not yet ready to stand by themselves under the strenuous conditions of the modern world . . . form a sacred trust of civilization." The permanent commission was to examine these annual reports and to "advise the Council on all matters relating to the observance of the mandates." The Council was given no power to execute the advice proffered by

[1]Russia had also signed secret agreements, but Russia was not represented at the peace conference.

[2]For the full text of article 22 as well as of articles 3, 4, 10, 11, 21 and 23, see the appendix, pp. 103-104.

the commission. Moreover, the Council was dominated by the colonial powers, mandatory and non-mandatory. It is to be noted also that while certain prohibitions were spelled out, the only positive freedom stipulated was that of conscience or religion. Nothing specific was said concerning the education, health, labor or political development of the Native inhabitants of the Class B and C mandates. Finally, largely because of pressure from opponents of the Covenant, acceptance of a mandate was made voluntary.[3]

The inhabitants of the Turkish communities to be placed under mandate were considered to be already sufficiently advanced so that only a provisional period of tutelage was deemed necessary. These Turkish communities came to be called Class A mandates.

But the inhabitants of the German colonies in Central Africa were deemed so backward that an indefinite period of tutelage was envisaged during which the mandatory would be responsible for carrying out the "sacred trust." The mandatory was also to secure "equal opportunities for the trade and commerce of other members of the League" in these Class B mandates.

South-West Africa and the Pacific islands taken from Germany, because of their scant population, small size, remoteness of contiguity to the mandatory, "and other circumstances," could be best administered as integral parts of its territory. While the same safeguards were assured to these Class C mandates as to the Class B, the former were not to enjoy the equality of opportunities for trade and commerce stipulated for the latter.

It can be argued that the surrender of the German colonies to the Principal Allied and Associated Powers under the Treaty of Versailles violated Wilson's Fifth Point which had stated: "A free, open-minded, and absolutely impartial adjustment of all colonial claims, based upon a strict observance of the princi-

---

[3]The standard American work is Quincy Wright, *Mandates under the League of Nations* (Chicago, 1930). See also Logan, *The Operation of the Mandate System in Africa, 1919-1927 with an Introduction on the Problem of the Mandates in the Post-War World* (Washington, 1942).

ple that in determining all such questions of sovereignty the interests of the populations concerned must have equal weight with the equitable claims of the government whose title is to be determined." Whatever equitable claims Germany may have had were disregarded—in fact, she had no opportunity of presenting them for she was not allowed to participate in the Paris negotiations. When the Germans on May 9, 1919, submitted a counter-draft to the proposed treaty in which they suggested an international administration for all colonies not ready for self-government, their proposal was categorically rejected.

The African possessions of Germany placed under mandate were the Cameroons, divided between France and Britain; Togoland, likewise divided between France and Britain; Tanganyika, allotted to Britain; Ruanda Urundi, to Belgium; and South-West Africa to the Union of South Africa. They covered an area of about 932,000 square miles and had a population of about twelve millions. They had not been greatly developed by Germany, for their export and import trade each constituted less than one per cent of the total German foreign trade. Only about 20,000 Germans lived in them in 1913.[4] At that time they were not considered to have much strategic value. Most of the inhabitants, regardless of the tortuous conclusions of some anthropologists, would certainly be considered Negroes by Americans. Not even the most persuasive anthropologist could truthfully assert that they had reached a degree of civilization comparable to that of the western nations although not all of them were the debased cannibalistic savages depicted by most popular writers.

The Pacific possessions of Germany consisted of the Marshall, Caroline and Marianne Islands, lying north of the equator; Western Samoa, German New Guinea and a group of islands including Nauru, lying south of the equator. These covered about 96,160 square miles with a population of some 357,800. They likewise had little economic value except Nauru which was an important source of phosphates and only some 1,500

---

[4]*Statesman's Year Book, 1913* (London, 1913), pp. 890-895.

Germans had settled in them.[5] Since Japan was on "our side" in the first world war, the strategic importance of these "stepping stones" did not impinge upon the minds of many Americans. There was, however, a little discussion in the Senate of their strategic importance. The Native inhabitants have varying degrees of Negro and Polynesian blood. Most of them were even more primitive than the inhabitants of the German possessions in Africa. The Marshall, Caroline and Marianne Islands were mandated to Japan, Western Samoa to New Zealand, German New Guinea and the islands lying south of the equator to Australia except Nauru which was allotted to Britain.

The distribution of the German colonies was made on May 7, 1919, largely on the basis of the existing occupation and the secret treaties. The date is significant since it preceded the signing of the Treaty of Versailles on June 28, 1919, of which the Covenant was an integral part, and the White House conference of August 19, 1919 when Wilson was questioned about the distribution.[6]

The Turkish possessions were finally assigned on April 25, 1920. Syria and the Lebanon were allotted to France, Mesopotamia (Iraq), Palestine and Trans-Jordan to Britain. They had an area of about 330,000 square miles and a population of some six and a half millions, mostly Arabs. One author contends that their oil resources were the principal reason for the interest of the mandatories in them,[7] but the Senate debates reveal also their strategic importance, especially of Armenia where the conflict between the Cross and the Crescent gave senators an opportunity for many rhetorical flights. The Senate, nevertheless, rejected Wilson's request that the United States accept a mandate for Armenia.[8] Thus the nation whose chief executive had been primarily responsible for the establishment

---

[5]*Ibid.*, pp., 895-897.

[6]See below, pp. 51-54.

[7]Lester C. Uren, "The Struggle for Oil in the Near East," in University of California, Los Angeles, ed., *Africa, the Near East and the War* (Berkeley and Los Angeles, 1943), p. 87. For the statistics, see *Statesman's Year Book, 1913*, pp. 1305 ff.

[8]See below, pp. 97-102.

of the mandate system refused to become mandatory for even a "white, Christian" people.

The mandate system was first embodied in the Covenant as article 17 on February 10, 1919. It became article 19 on February 13; article 21 on April 11 and finally article 22 on April 21. Acceptance of a mandate was made voluntary on April 28, the day on which the Covenant was adopted. The entire treaty was signed by Germany on June 28.[9]

The Senate debates on article 22 can no more be considered *in vacuo* than can any other articles since it was a part of the Covenant and the Covenant was an integral part of the Treaty. This fact is especially true since discussion of articles 3, 10, 11, 21, 23 and the labor provisions in Part XIII frequently revealed significant attitudes with respect to the mandated areas. Article 3 gave each member of the League an equal vote. Article 10, "the heart of the Covenant" as Wilson generally termed it, provided that the Council should "advise" upon the means by which the members would "undertake to respect and preserve as against external aggression the territorial integrity and existing political independence of all Members of the League." Under article 11 the League was called upon to take any action that it deemed "wise and effectual to safeguard the peace of nations." Article 21 dealt with the Monroe Doctrine. Article 23 was a general provision looking to the improvement of social and economic conditions.

Above all, the debates must be analyzed against the background of the bitter political rivalry between Republicans and Democrats, the personal hostility of Lodge, Republican chairman of the Committee on Foreign Relations, the almost perennial conflict between the Senate and the president over the treaty-making power, and the strong feeling of isolation which has been one of the themes of American foreign policy. Denna F. Fleming and W. Stull Holt[10] have made excellent analyses of this background, but even Fleming gave scant attention and

[9]David Hunter Miller, *The Drafting of the Covenant* (New York, 1928), *passim.*

[10]Fleming, *The United States and the League of Nations, 1918-1920* (New York, 1932); Holt, Chapter X in his *Treaties Defeated by the Senate* (Baltimore, 1933).

space to the discussions of the mandates. Consequently, the following observations and conclusions are mostly original.

Most of the opponents of the League were generally bitter, even vituperative in their attacks upon articles 3, 10, 11, 21, 22 and 23, and the labor provisions. The defenders only mildly favored them especially articles 22 and 23. The reasons for this mild enthusiasm are, I believe, easily understandable. Articles 22 and 23 contained the most significant humanitarian provisions, and the majority of the peoples covered by them as well as by article 10 were Negroes and other dark peoples. Now, many of the most powerful Democratic members in the Senate were from the South, the section where Negroes and labor in general were most flagrantly exploited. John Sharp Williams of Mississippi, for example, a leader in the fight for the treaty, was one of the most rabid race-baiters of the era. In the "most august deliberative assembly in the world," he did not hesitate to refer to Negroes as "darkies" and "niggers." On one occasion he attempted to justify the lynching of what he called "the miserable black beast." McKellar of Tennessee had inserted into the *Record* an article declaring that the true basis of white supremacy was not brutality but service to the Negro. At all events, the article continued, " 'America is now a white man's country, and a white man's country I hope it remains.' "[11]

Since Williams and McKellar were advocates of the League, they had to put a bridle generally upon their real feelings with respect to race and labor. Williams had so many newspaper articles inserted that Fall dubbed him "the exchange editor." But Reed, an irreconcilable Democrat from the border state of Missouri, pulled out all the stops. During a colloquy with another senator Reed said that he was "not talking of bootleggers or of niggers playing craps in an alley." One of Reed's favorite rhetorical flights depicted the League as being dominated by the "inferior" dark nations. His attitude toward dark peoples was clearly revealed in a debate on immigration in which he sneered: "The Moors from Morocco can come in

[11]*Congressional Record,* 66th Cong., 1st sess., pp. 1554, 2610, 6080; 66th Cong., 2nd sess., pp. 967-968.

[under the proposed legislation]; the polite and cultured inhabitant of Algeria is welcomed with open arms; the individual who inhabits darkest Abyssinia is a highly desirable immigrant, we open our arms to embrace him; the civilized and cultured denizen of Madagascar is invited to come; the intellectual bushman of the Congo is eagerly sought." In this same speech he asserted that "wherever the white race exists men and women have been capable of setting up civilization, of achieving everything that is glorious and beautiful in civilization."[12]

Of course not all Democrats, whether from the North, the South or border states, gave vent to their real feelings. But the Southerners represented constituencies in which Negroes were almost completely disfranchised by legal, extra-legal and illegal means; where there had been an average of about sixty lynchings between 1913 and 1918; where the per capita expenditure for the education of white children was several times that for colored; where the great majority of the Negroes were exploited workers on plantations and in private homes; where segregation was as fixed a pattern as it was in 1943 when a Southern "Liberal," Mark Ethridge, declared:

> There is no power in the world—not even in all the mechanized armies of the earth, Allied and Axis—which could now force the Southern white people to the abandonment of the principle of social segregation.[13]

Not much enthusiasm could be expected, then, from Southern senators for a treaty that made the welfare of dark peoples a "sacred trust of civilization," especially if the treaty involved spending American money and sending American "boys" to die all over the world.

Moreover, the South represented a region in which not only black but also white workers were exploited. The latest biographer of Henry W. Grady, the eloquent advocate of the "New South," in his attempt to show the Georgian a friend of labor presents on the other hand evidence that Grady did use the

---

[12] *Ibid.*, 64th Cong., 2nd sess., p. 2620; 66th Cong., 1st sess., pp. 235 ff., 1449, 6028-6029.

[13] Quoted by John Temple Graves, *The Fighting South* (New York, 1943), p. 125. For conditions in the South see Gunnar Myrdal, with the assistance of Richard Sterner and Arnold Rose, *An American Dilemma* (New York and London, 1944), *passim;* Arthur Raper, *The Tragedy of Lynching* (Chapel Hill, 1933), pp. 480-481.

appeal of cheap white labor as one of the best arguments for the industrialization of the South.[14] Not much support for article 23 and for an International Labor Organization could be looked for from senators who spoke for the "New South" and even less from those who still considered the Old South a paradise for white men.

In 1917-1920 the cleavage between Southern and Northern Democrats which has characterized intra-party politics since the inception of the New Deal was not pronounced. Consequently, the Northern Democrats were compelled to maintain solidarity with their Southern colleagues on these points on which Southerners were adamant.

These racial and economic attitudes of Southerners may offer a clue to the enigma as to why they so readily followed Wilson's lead in rejecting the treaty with reservations. I have the suspicion that they really wanted the treaty defeated with or without reservations.

While most of the Southern Democrats and their sympathisers were generally only mildly in favor of the pertinent articles, the Republicans were frequently vituperative in their denunciation of them. The debates therefore reveal two anomalies: the party which had to support the greatest humanitarian document presented to the Senate was most contemptuous of human rights and the party determined to defeat it was the traditional "friend" of the Negro. On the other hand, the Republican party represented the conservative vested economic interests that were no more friendly to labor than were the Southern Democrats. Inasmuch as national interests and world peace were subordinated by the Republicans to partisanship and personalism, it is not surprising that "friendship" for the Negro, which had been in part at least dictated by regular support of Northern Negroes in elections, was subordinated to the paramount objective, defeat of the treaty. The Republicans had no great concern for the dark peoples in other parts of the world.

---

[14] See the author's review of Raymond B. Nixon's *Henry W. Grady, Spokesman of the New South* (New York, 1943) in *Journal of Negro Education*, XII (No. 4, 1944), 522-524.

Just as they had abandoned the Southern Negro to the "New South," just so they saw no reason for obligating the United States to protect dark peoples in far-distant lands. A cynic would add that they had even less since these latter did not vote in American elections.

The most outspoken "humanitarians" were three irreconcilables, Borah and France, Republicans, and Thomas, Democrat.[15] The irreconcilables first voted for reservations and then voted against the treaty after these reservations had been added.

Rarely, then, has the vote on a treaty presented so many anomalies. Political partisanship, bitter personal hatreds, the persistent conflict between the senate and the president, and the "entirely proper"[16] issue of isolation have been emphasized by all writers on the subject. The reader may determine for himself the extent to which race and labor were openly expressed or latent factors in the defeat of the Treaty of Versailles which prevented the United States from joining the League of Nations.

---

[15]*Congressional Record,* 65th Cong., 3rd sess., pp. 237-240, 999, 4967-5003; 66th Cong., 1st sess., pp. 6077, 6331.

[16]Holt, *Treaties Defeated by the Senate,* p. 306.

Chapter II

64TH CONGRESS, 2ND SESSION, 65TH CONGRESS, 1ST AND 2ND SESSIONS

The Senate discussed at some length problems affecting the later mandated areas during the more than two calendar years that preceded the crucial sessions of 1919 and 1920. These discussions were generally provoked by statements in Wilson's addresses, especially his emphasis upon the principle of the "consent of the governed."[1] Not once, however, did Wilson specifically apply the principle to the inhabitants of the later mandated areas and not once did he outline a plan for the future administration of these regions. It is not surprising, then, that senators made no such application or plan. The Democrats followed the president's lead. The Republicans, although Lodge (Republican, Massachusetts) promised that "this is not, and can not be, a party war,"[2] were largely engaged in sniping at the president's proposals. Since the Republicans were in a minority in the 64th and 65th Congresses, they felt no responsibility for formulating a foreign policy.

The first important discussion resulted from Wilson's memorable address to the Senate on January 22, 1917. In it he proposed a league of nations, a world court, freedom of the seas, free outlet to the seas, disarmament, and uttered his famous phrase that there must be a "peace without victory." But he also asserted that "no peace can last, or ought to last, which does not recognize and accept the principle that governments derive their just powers from the consent of the governed and that no right anywhere exists to hand peoples about from sovereignty to sovereignty as if they were property." He was convinced that these ideals were a fulfilment of all the high and honorable hopes of the American people.[3]

---

[1]The Declaration of Independence stated that "governments derive all their just powers from the consent of the governed." For the general origins of Wilson's foreign policy see Harley Notter, *The Origins of the Foreign Policy of Woodrow Wilson* (Baltimore, 1937).

[2]*Congressional Record*, 65th Cong., 1st sess., p. 207.

[3]*Ibid.*, 64th Cong., 2nd sess., pp. 1741-1743.

Two days later the Senate gave early evidence of the partisanship which later became fatal. Sherman (Republican irreconcilable, Illinois) called the address a "stump speech from the throne," while Hoke Smith (Democrat, Georgia) praised it effusively. No senator at first deemed worthy of discussion Wilson's idealistic principles of consent of the governed and no bartering of peoples as though they were property. On January 20 Cummins (Republican, Iowa) made many of the charges that later became the stock in trade of the opposition. "It was proposed," he charged, "that we shall surrender our sovereignty, transfer to a new nation or league our Army, our Navy, and with them our Treasury, to put at the disposal of a power higher than our own the lives and fortunes of our men and women, to make the former fight and the latter suffer when commanded by an alien authority." He derided the principle of the consent of the governed which could be made to apply, he pointed out, not only to Europe, Asia Minor, India and Latin America but even to the Boers in South Africa. It is thus evident that this midwestern Republican could not conceive that the principle had any application to the German colonies in Africa or the Pacific but that he did consider them pertinent to the Turkish possessions. Quite inconsistently, however, he quoted from an article by Albert Bushnell Hart in the *New York Times* of January 28 in which the Harvard historian charged that a general peace would maintain the *status quo* and queried: " 'Who is to give reasonable play to the irregular development of nations, to the growth of race elements inside of countries, to the rising of great communities out of the colonial States?' " Senator Hitchcock (Democrat, Nebraska), Chairman of the Senate Committee on Foreign Relations, insisted that the address was not before the Senate since it had not been referred to that Committee. Borah (Republican irreconcilable, Idaho) seized the occasion to emphasize the treaty-making power of the Senate. Hitchcock declared that the moral force of a league would be sufficient to preserve the peace of the world which, he believed, would depend upon self-government and upon the "publicity of diplomacy." He made no specific application of the principle of self-government.[4]

On February 1 McCumber (Republican, North Dakota, who was the only member of his party to vote for the treaty with reservations) introduced a resolution expressing disagreement with *any* of the matters listed by the president as conditions precedent to the entrance of the United States into a league. He was, however, in general accord with the idea of a league. He was sure that the American people were as desirous of rescuing the Armenians from atrocities committed by the Turks as they were of liberating Poland. He asked bluntly whether the president, in accordance with his principle of self-government, proposed as a condition precedent to American participation in a league that Great Britain should relinquish her African and Asiatic possessions, or her rule over Ireland if the inhabitants of those countries should so desire. It went without saying, he asserted, that the territorial limits including those of the colonial possessions would have to be determined before a world congress could even be proposed. He also injected the color question which, he contended, would have to be discussed in the conclave of nations unless it was to be exclusively a combination of white races. "The rights of the yellow people to become citizens of white nations must be settled," he warned, "and settled to the satisfaction of the yellow people themselves before they will become parties to the compact."[5]

Lodge, Wilson's implacable foe and later Chairman of the Committee on Foreign Relations, insisted that there would have to be a victory in order to get the kind of government that Wilson wanted. He inquired, probably with sarcasm, whether the consent of the governed would be determined by popular vote or by the general acceptance of the people of the existing form of government. If the principle were applied, what was to be done about Korea, Hindustan, Alsace-Lorraine, Trentino, the Slav provinces of Austria, the Danish duchies, Armenia? What

---

[4]*Ibid.*, 64th Cong., 2nd sess., pp. 1884-1885, 2230-2239.
[5]*Ibid.*, 64th Cong., 2nd sess., pp. 2361-2364.

also about Louisiana, California, the Philippines, Puerto Rico, and Alaska? (He did not mention Haiti or the Dominican Republic, then occupied by American marines.) He attacked, as had McCumber, Wilson's other conditions precedent. He too introduced a statement by Professor Hart which estimated that the maintenance of peace would require a force of 5,000,-000 of which the United States would have to furnish 500,000. Were the American people ready to have their army and navy inspected and reported upon regularly by officers of foreign nations? He rang the changes on isolation, painted the spectre of Japanese immigration into Canada, Australia, New Zealand and the United States and made the plea that the United States first of all prepare her own defense. At the close of his peroration there was applause in the galleries. Senator Thomas (Democratic irreconcilable, Colorado), who warmly supported Wilson's conditions precedent, applied the principle of self-determination to the restoration of white "home rule" in the South after the American Civil War and the liberal treatment accorded to the Boers in South Africa.[6]

Wilson in his address to both Houses on February 3, in which he announced the severance of diplomatic relations with Germany, reiterated that "we wish to serve no selfish aims" and that he stood on the principles of January 22. The debate on February 7 revealed that there was no desire for territorial aggrandizement. The president, in his joint message of February 26, again renounced any selfish claims and proclaimed again "that righteous passion for justice upon which all law, all structures alike of family, of state, of mankind must rest."[7]

At the opening of the special session of the Senate of the 65th Congress on March 5 Wilson repeated in his inaugural message that "governments derive all their just powers from the consent of the governed." In his war message of April 2 at the opening of the first session of this Congress he declared that his thoughts were the same as they had been in his messages

---

[6] *Ibid.*, 64th Cong., 2nd sess., pp. 2364-2371. *Cf.* Karl Schriftgiesser, *The Gentleman from Massachusetts: Henry Cabot Lodge* (Boston, 1944), p. 289 and ff.

[7] *Congressional Record*, 64th Cong., 2nd sess., pp. 2550, 2729-2749, 4272-4273.

of January 22, February 23 and 26. Hitchcock in discussing on April 4 the joint resolution declaring a state of war between the United States and Germany contrasted the explicit and implicit altruism of the United States with the conquests of Britain who had almost within her grasp the German commerce and colonies. Lodge insisted that the American people were entering the war to unite with those who "are fighting the common foe in order to preserve human freedom, democracy, and modern civilization." Myers (Democrat, Montana) added that the United States sought to secure for the "struggling, panting world" some of the rights which Americans had long exclusively enjoyed. La Follette (Republican irreconcilable, Wisconsin) on the other hand criticized Wilson's assertion that the war was being fought for democracy, for the president had not suggested that the United States make her support of Britain conditional upon the granting of "home rule" to Ireland, India and Egypt.[8] But not even this famous Liberal referred to the colonies of the allies or of the enemy. There is nothing in the sixty pages of debate to indicate any interest in or desire for the German colonies. Nor was there in the debate on the issuance of bonds as a credit to the allies on April 17 anything to suggest that the German colonies captured by the British Commonwealth should be turned over to the United States.[9]

Indeed, Lewis (Democrat, Illinois) believed, July 23, that peace should be made on the basis of the *status quo ante bellum* including the return of the German colonies. But McCumber on the same day stated that he had gleaned from Lloyd George's statements that the prime minister was willing to allow the inhabitants of the German colonies to determine for themselves the country to which they would be attached.[10] The colonial question, according to McCumber, should not therefore present any difficulty. The Pope in his appeal of August 1, 1917, made a plea for reciprocal restitution of territory then

[8] *Ibid.*, 65th Cong., special and 1st sess., pp. 3, 102-104, 201, 208, 223, 228.

[9] *Ibid.*, 65th Cong., 1st sess., pp. 228-393.

[10] See, for example, Lloyd George's speech early in 1917 as reported in *Parliamentary Debates*, vol. 100, p. 2220.

occupied including specifically the German colonies. The Executive Committee of the Union of Democratic Control (England) demanded categorically that Britain should definitely repudiate any claims to annex them. It further insisted that while changes might be made to have them conform to the Berlin Act of 1885, Germany was "not less entitled than other great powers to organize and develop overseas dependencies."[11]

The printing of these two appeals aroused no more interest than had the statements of Lewis and McCumber. Two of the passages in Wilson's reply of August 27 to the Pope, printed in the *Record* on August 29, only vaguely had some reference to the colonial problem. One declared that "peace should rest upon the rights of peoples great or small, weak or powerful—their equal right to freedom and security and self-government and to participation upon fair terms in the economic opportunities of the world." The other pointed out that the United States deemed "punitive damages, the dismemberment of empires, the establishment of selfish and exclusive economic leagues . . . inexpedient and in the end worse than futile." It is obvious, of course, that the dismemberment of the colonial empires might be necessary to secure self-government for the inhabitants, but there is no certainty that Wilson meant the colonial empires. The term German Empire, for example, was currently used to describe only Germany in Europe. While the *Washington Post* praised Wilson for his second plea, the excerpts printed in the *Record* from New York, Boston, Philadelphia and Baltimore papers made no reference to the colonial question. There was no discussion of the president's message or of the newspaper extracts.[12]

Nor did Wilson's Fifth of his Fourteen Points of January 8, 1918 seem to create any interest among senators at that time. It stipulated "A free, open-minded, and absolutely impartial

[11]*Congressional Record*, 65th Cong., 1st sess., pp. 5383-5385, 6252-6254. The Berlin Act promised to protect the Natives of Africa and provided for freedom of trade and equal treatment of the commerce of all nations between the fifth degree North latitude and the Zambesi River. Among the signers of the London statement were Norman Angell, J. A. Hobson, E. L. Morel, Charles Trevelyan, Charles R. Buxton, F. W. Jowett, and J. Ramsay MacDonald.

[12]*Ibid.*, 65th Cong., 1st sess., pp. 6407-6409.

adjustment of all colonial claims, based upon a strict observance of the principle that in determining all such questions of sovereignty the interests of the populations concerned must have equal weight with the equitable claims of the government whose title is to be determined." He had previously asserted that "the day of conquest and aggrandizement is gone by." Subsequently he declared: "We have no jealousy of German greatness, and there is nothing in this program that impairs it. We grudge her no achievement or distinction of learning or of pacific enterprise such as have made her record very bright and very enviable. We do not wish to injure her or to block in any way her legitimate influence or power. . . . We wish her only to accept a place of equality among the peoples of the world—the new world in which we now live—instead of a place of mastery." Quite clearly there was room here for German imperialists to build up a case for the retention of their colonies although Wilson did not specifically mention them. The president in his closing paragraph asserted that the "principle of justice to all peoples and nationalities" ran through every point.[13]

After the Central Powers had replied on January 24 to Wilson's address of January 8 and Lloyd George's address of January 5,[14] Wilson again appeared before both Houses on February 11. Von Hertling's reply, he stated, was very vague and confusing. On one point, however, the German chancellor had been very specific: the German colonies "must be returned without debate." The president laid down four principles, three of which might have been applicable to the colonial question as follows:

> First, that each part of the final settlement must be based upon the essential justice of that particular case and upon such adjustments as are most likely to bring a peace that will be permanent;
>
> Second, that peoples and provinces are not to be bartered about from sovereignty to sovereignty as if they were mere chattels and pawns in a

[13]*Ibid.*, 65th Cong., 2nd sess., pp. 680-681.

[14]The prime minister had specifically stated that "the general principle of national self determination is as applicable in the cases of the German colonies as in those of occupied European territories."—David Lloyd George, *War Memoirs of David Lloyd George* (London, 1933-1936), V, 2485-2489.

game, even the great game, now forever discredited, of the balance of power; but that

Third, every territorial settlement involved in this war must be made in the interest and for the benefit of the populations concerned, and not as a part of any mere adjustment or compromise of claims amongst rival States; . . .

Wilson further elaborated his peace aims at Mount Vernon on July 4 when he declared *inter alia:*

II. The settlement of every question, whether of territory, of sovereignty, of economic arrangement, or of political relationship, upon the basis of the free acceptance of that settlement by the people immediately concerned, and not upon the basis of the material interest or advantage of any other nation or people which may desire a different settlement for the sake of its own exterior influence or mastery.[15]

None of these statements immediately elicited any discussion in the Senate.

Lodge's peace aims, given in the Senate on August 23, included the assertions that "we intend to make the world safe for democracy"[16] and that the allies were fighting for the right of "organized races and peoples to have the opportunity to govern themselves in independent States." (Since the Massachusetts senator had no reason for thinking that the Natives of Africa or the Pacific islands were "organized," there was no inconsistency in his proposal that Belgium might be compensated by the acquisition of the German colonies.) He was one of the first to develop the German "colonial guilt" theme when he said that the colonies should never be "returned to the Empire which has abused all the ordinary rights of humanity." McCumber repeated the charge in more detail on September 17 after the Kaiser had declared that the responsible leaders of the German government had been ready "at all times to offer the hand of peace." After excoriating Germany in blistering terms and praising British colonial administration, he asserted that while Britain was "loved and defended in her every possession, you [Germany] are hated and feared [in yours]."[17]

---

[15]*Congressional Record,* 65th Cong., 2nd sess., pp. 1936-1937, 11,172.

[16]Wilson had used this expression in his war message.

[17]*Congressional Record,* 65th Cong., 2nd sess., pp. 9392-9396, 10,401-10,403. For a different view of Germany's colonial administration see Harry R. Rudin, *Germans in the Cameroons 1884-1914* (New Haven, 1938).

Rather long discussions of peace terms on October 7 and 10 revealed no interest in the colonial question. On October 14, however, New (Republican, Indiana) in a brief statement reminded the Senate that the United States had desired no colonies on *entering the war*. But the heavy losses of eighteen months had convinced him that the American people would "not unwittingly or complacently submit to seeing themselves placed at a permanent and irremediable commercial disadvantage through the medium of peace." He did not, nevertheless, make a specific demand for compensation in the form of German colonies. Although Cummins listed Draconian terms of peace, he did not refer to the colonies. McCumber was the only Senator who spoke on that day to mention them. One of the terms of the Central Powers after their onslaught of March 21, 1918, had given them some hope of victory was the restitution to Germany of all her colonies.[18]

In the terms of the armistice of November 11 the only reference to the German colonies was the stipulation that all German forces operating in East Africa should surrender in one month. Wilson, commenting upon the hostilities in Europe, asserted that "armed imperialism" was at an end and that the victorious nations were determined to make a peace that would satisfy the longing of the world "for disinterested justice, embodied in settlements which are based upon something better and much more lasting than the competitive interests of powerful states. . . . Their avowed and concerted purpose is to satisfy and protect the weak as well as to accord their just rights to the strong."[19]

When Walsh (Democrat, Montana) announced on November 15 his support of a league but stated that at that time no one could make an exact statement as to its powers, Penrose (Republican, Pennsylvania) ridiculed the idea of a league as

[18]*Congressional Record,* 65th Cong., 2nd sess., pp. 11,155-11,181, 11,204-11,213, 11,214-11,220, 11,225.

[19]*Ibid.,* 65th Cong., 2nd sess., pp. 11,537-11,539.

being "nebulous" and a "kind of rainbow vision." The debate wandered off into a discussion of the extent to which munitions makers controlled the press in various countries, the views of H. G. Wells, the Monroe Doctrine, the loss of sovereignty if the United States entered the league.[20]

Owen had printed without reading a number of resolutions which he had introduced at various times since August 15, 1917, for the purpose of "establishing an international government in lieu of the international anarchy which was then and is still prevalent." The first stipulated:

> Every civilized nation and informed people should have the unquestionable right of internal self-government. . . . Nations backward in education, industrial and economic development, and in the knowledge of the principles of government should have their rights safeguarded on the principles of freedom, humanity and justice by international agreement, with a view to future self-government.

Owen obviously used the word nations in a vague sense. If by nations backward in education, he meant independent nations, they would already possess self-government. If he meant by the expression peoples, then he was among the first to propose in the Senate international machinery for the purpose of promoting their self-government.

It is possible that Owen had dependent peoples in mind, for in his second resolution he urged the United States to favor "safeguarding the rights of backward peoples by international agreement." This second resolution also contained a provision that is exceedingly interesting in view of the discussions at San Francisco of the administration of strategic areas "detached from the enemy." Owen suggested that

> dissatisfied peoples now held under subjection to dominating nations for strategical purposes could be safely given their liberty and autonomy as the rights of the dominant nation would be made safe by the general association of nations, and the subject nation would cease to be a coveted asset against future war.

---

[20] *Ibid.*, 65th Cong., 2nd sess., pp. 11,560-11,565.

But once more Owen had used the words peoples and nations interchangeably. His third resolution was, however, explicit. It specified:

> Subordinate nations or colonies, backward in education and in industrial and economic development, should have their human rights safeguarded on the principles of freedom and justice by international agreement.

Unfortunately, Owen did not in his rather long discourse discuss either the principles or the machinery sufficiently to give any clear idea of exactly what he had in mind. Nor did any senator consider the proposals important enough to reveal his thinking on the subject. Perhaps they were awaiting Wilson's leadership. Owen closed his speech with an eloquent but very vague plea for the United States to "take the lead in establishing on earth the doctrines of humanity, democracy, of the people's rule system of government."[21]

On the last day of the session Reed made a highly emotional plea in behalf of isolationism. This was the first speech in which he sneered at small nations, especially Haiti, Liberia and Serbia. Was the United States, he sarcastically inquired, to have the same representation as these nations? He also read the list of royal houses of Europe to show the extent to which kinship and marriage tied them together. What chance would the United States have with a court dominated by these in-laws, he pointedly suggested. Moreover, England, France and Germany had absorbed practically all of Africa, and Germany and England had looked with "ambitious and greedy eyes" toward South America. It may be doubted that he was thinking of colonial subjects when he criticized a league because under it no oppressed people would be able to rebel since they would have to fight not only the "unjust government of their own State, but . . . the governments of all the other countries of the league." He pointed out the differences in civilizations of the nations that would make up the league—"pagan" China and Japan and the " 'unspeakable Turk.' "[22]

---

[21] *Ibid.*, 65th Cong., 2nd sess., pp. 11,567-11,571.
[22] *Ibid.*, 65th Cong., 2nd sess., pp. 11,622-11,624.

This preview of the crucial debates from May, 1919 to March, 1920 manifested little concern for the fate of the inhabitants of the German colonies, but it did reveal considerable interest in Armenia, Ireland and India in all of which the principle of the consent of the governed was involved. This rehearsal of the great drama illustrates that quirk of American statesmen that permits them to quote the most altruistic general principles with mental reservations as to their application. The historian can only record the phenomenon; a psychiatrist may be able to explain them.

Chapter III

SIXTY-FIFTH CONGRESS, THIRD SESSION

The third session of the 65th Congress heard rumblings of the negotiations in Paris that produced premonitory thunders of the brewing storm. Wilson opened the session on December 2, 1918 with the significant statement that the Allied and Central Powers had accepted the bases of peace which he had outlined in his Fourteen Points of January 8, 1918. He informed Congress that the allies "very reasonably" desired his personal counsel in their interpretation and application. He promised to stay in close touch with Congress which would know all that he did, and he asked for their "encouragement and the added strength" of their united support.[1]

But now the bitter partisanship of the Republicans, increased by Wilson's appeal for party support during the Congressional elections and by his failure to appoint a Republican delegate fully acceptable to Lodge, became openly manifest. On the second day of the session Sherman offered a resolution declaring the office of president vacant if Wilson went to Paris, and Knox (Republican irreconcilable, Pennsylvania) offered a resolution declaring that the peace conference should be confined to making the peace and "matters germane thereto" and that "any project for a general league of nations . . . should be postponed for separate consideration."[2]

Walsh on the following day, December 4, sought to obtain support for Wilson's peace aims by stating that although they had been published on January 8, only in the preceding six weeks did he have any recollection of a member of the Senate expressing any divergence from them. Poindexter (Republican irreconcilable, Washington) interrupted to say that he like others had kept quiet until the war had been won. Hiram Johnson (Republican irreconcilable, California) stated that several senators had expressed their satisfaction when the president in

[1] *Congressional Record,* 65th Cong., 3rd sess., pp. 5-8.
[2] *Ibid.,* 65th Cong., 3rd sess., p. 23.

his February address had modified somewhat the January address. Lewis pointed out that the Senate had devoted no real thought to any of the peace terms including the disposition of the German colonies. Reed in a long discourse gave further evidence of his Negrophobia and xenophobia.[3]

Lewis on December 6 made a typical speech in support of the league without mentioning the colonial problem. Borah almost instantly proclaimed his opposition to a league because any "practical league of nations means that we are to enter into entangling alliances in Europe, and all Europe and all Asia and all Africa." Williams repeated the German "colonial guilt" theme. Lodge on December 10 revealed his interest in the Turkish possessions when he inserted into the *Record* an article stating that the lands under Turkish rule should be freed and their governments organized in conformity with racial conditions and under the protection of the allied powers. With respect to the German colonies he limited himself to the statement that they were not to be returned to Germany. Shafroth (Democrat, Colorado) had printed a speech in which Thomas called attention to lynchings and labor disputes in the United States when German brutalities were being denounced.[4]

After the Senate had discussed the income tax law for a week, Knox on December 18 made a long speech in support of his resolution. As a part of the guaranty of Germany's "relative impotence" in the future he proposed that the German colonies should not be returned but should be divided among the chief belligerents, "with their respective authority somewhat proportioned to their respective local interests and to their positions as factors in victory." He further proposed that the raw materials from the tropical and other territories of the allies should be determined and apportioned as "they found convenient after supplying their own requirements and having in view to give Germany the means of subsistence but not the means of aggrandizement." After discussing the Monroe Doctrine and asking why the United States was in a hurry to get into a league, he

[3] *Ibid.*, 65th Cong., 3rd sess., pp. 70-71, 80-91.
[4] *Ibid.*, 65th Cong., 3rd sess., pp. 178-199, 237-240.

warned that the United States could not "nurse every backward nation. The most we can do," he thought, "is to strive to give favorable opportunity to evolution. It may be that we shall have to guard against letting the phrase 'self-determination' quite run away with us." There is no evidence that Knox was thinking about the German colonies or the Turkish possessions in this connection. He strongly leaned in the direction of regionalism (but without any overall international authority), with Britain dominant in India and the Near East "and vastly interested in Africa," and "the sphere of the United States conformed primarily to the regions affected by the Monroe Doctrine."[5]

Pittman (Democrat, Nevada) accused Knox of failing to make a distinction between the reasons that had led the United States to enter the war and the aspirations of the United States in making peace. He quoted from Wilson's speech of June 14, 1917, in which the president had said that the United States was fighting for "the rights of nations great and small and the privilege of men *everywhere* to choose their way of life and obedience." But like most other speakers he made no application of the principle to colonial subjects.[6]

Lodge in a long discourse on December 21 argued that the first step was to make a peace with Germany that would prevent her from attempting again to conquer the world. He favored putting Constantinople under international protection with Greece perhaps as mandatory. This seems to have been the first time the word mandatory was used in the Senate. While he did not propose a mandatory for the German colonies, he did demand again that they should not be returned to the "tyrannical" government of Germany, which should be deprived of using them for building up her commercial and military strength. He asked further whether senators believed that the United States could insist that Europe recognize the "hands-off" policy of the United States without a similar demand by the

[5]*Ibid.*, 65th Cong., 3rd sess., pp. 602-605.
[6]*Ibid.*, 65th Cong., 3rd sess., pp. 606-609. Italics not in the original.

European nations that a "great circle" be drawn around Africa, Europe and Asia.[7]

McKellar on December 20, replying to Lodge and Knox, asserted that England, France and Italy would all want colonies. Like Wilson he declared that unless the league was formed before these problems had been settled, there would be the usual contest for the spoils of war. King (Democrat, Utah) interrupted him to say that England did not want any of the German colonies and had "besought" the United States to take the colonies or at least to devise some means by which they could be administered. McKellar agreed that while he had not seen the official statement, King was probably correct. Williams chimed in to add the assurance that the statement was "absolutely correct" save for the fact that the Union of South Africa wanted to hold on to South-West Africa.[8] Interestingly enough in view of what many persons undoubtedly believe to be an original contribution of this war, the *Record* used as a sub-headline during this discussion the words "A People's War; a People's Treaty."[9]

Lodge revealed more clearly his attitude toward the principle of self-determination when he inserted on January 3, 1919 a passage from H. G. Wells's *In the Fourth Year* in which the English author asked if under the principle Armenians in Constantinople, Jews in Roumania, Poles in West Prussia, Negroes in Georgia or Indians in the Transvaal could make a plea in the proposed supreme court of the world. On that same day Williams inserted Wilson's Guild Hall address of December 28 in which the president had spoken of the necessity for destroying the old concept of the balance of power and substituting for it "a single, powerful group of nations, who shall be *trustees* of the peace of the world."[10] One should not make the mistake, however, of believing that Williams or any other senator sub-

---

[7]*Ibid.*, 65th Cong., 3rd sess., pp. 725-728.

[8]In addition to the fact that these senators submitted no proof to substantiate their statements, Australia and New Zealand also wanted to keep their conquests.

[9]*Congressional Record,* 65th Cong., 3rd sess., pp. 921-925.

[10]*Ibid.*, 65th Cong., 3rd sess., pp. 972-973, 980. Italics not in the original.

scribed fully to every statement included in an article that he had printed in the *Record*.

Lewis, who had been absent because of illness on the day Knox had spoken, declared that what Knox was really asking was: " 'Mr. Wilson, please postpone yourself and postpone the Democratic Party and postpone any achievement and postpone any result, as we desire to postpone you perpetually.' " He queried what Britain, France and the other nations would do if the United States attempted to put Greece in control of the Dardanelles and Constantinople. Thomas asserted that all the peoples of the world were partners in the interest the peace-loving nations had in being able to live their own way of life without fear of force and selfish aggression such as Germany had employed. Germany, he asserted, had sought not only to secure the French and Belgian channel ports but also the French and British colonies and dependencies, "control of raw materials, world wide commercial supremacy, and freedom from international competition." He believed that the way to stop these trade wars was to remove economic barriers.[11]

McCumber on January 7 feared a league because of racial prejudices and of its attempt to assimilate "inferior races" which would lower the American standard of living. Contrary to Reed and others, he did not believe it necessary to invite Afghanistan, Paraguay or "every quarrelsome little country of Central America or Europe to join in this compact." The United States should make clear that, while she did not consider herself superior, she must build her national structure "on the foundations of Caucasian character and cement it with the purest of Caucasian blood." Thus this Republican enemy of the league spoke the same language as Southern supporters. He proposed a seven-point program for making peace, the third of which provided: "No nation shall forcibly annex any portion of any other nation, or claim or exercise control or suzerainty over it, or in any way limit its sovereign rights or independence." It may be doubted that he intended to apply this principle to the

---

[11]*Ibid.*, 65th Cong., 3rd sess., pp. 980-981, 994-999.

German colonies. Myers preferred postponing a league until after the treaty of peace had been signed. He favored severe punishment for Germany including the handing over of her colonies to Great Britain in part payment of the indemnity or the distribution of the colonies among the entente powers. Borah on January 14 advanced a favorite argument when he contended that the league advocated by the president would result in "the sending of American soldiers to Europe and Asia and Africa whenever any disturbance arises, although it may not affect our people at all." Cummins revealed his limited interest in the principle of self-government when he inquired on January 23 why the United States did nothing to promote self-determination in India.[12]

News of the controversy in Paris over the German colonies and of the secrecy with which the negotiations were being conducted was given the Senate on January 30 when Borah quoted from an article in the *New York Times* of the same date. It asserted that it was not " 'beyond the bounds of probability to say that the principle of internationalizing the German colonies, with a future administration intrusted to governments designated by the league of nations, will be recognized by the peace conference.' " The Idaho irreconcilable, instead of discussing the principle, condemned the secrecy. King protested that daily summaries would give information and that Borah could hardly expect the actual negotiations to be conducted in the presence of newspaper men. King understood that some of the allied governments wanted to govern them without reference to any league. Wilson and others, he understood, insisted that the "legal title" should be vested in the league and the "equitable title" in the various nations that would become "trustees." Did Borah decry the attempt to come to an agreement in the presence of newspaper men? Borah retorted that he certainly did. After considerable discussion of what constituted secret diplomacy, Kellogg (Republican, Minnesota) asked Borah whether he did not think that "one of the worst aspects of this case is

[12] *Ibid.*, 65th Cong., 3rd sess., pp. 1083-1088, 1318-1322, 1916.

any proposition emanating from any authority for this country to enter into a partnership to control African colonies and to operate them?" Borah replied that he was coming to that. Trusting his memory, he said that Mesopotamia and some of the countries in that region and especially Russia had been assigned to the United States. While the United States would get some of the German colonies as a "side diversion," America's principal task would be to restore order and sane government in Russia. What the United States was already doing in Russia[13] was an indication of what American boys would be called upon to do in Africa or Mesopotamia "if it so happened that under the league of nations in the assignments we were assigned to the possessions which Germany now has in Africa and other parts." He agreed with Johnson of California that the United States should look after her affairs at home. He categorically added: "I am utterly opposed to policing Russia, or policing Africa, or taking over under our control any part of the German colonies."[14]

Knox on the next day kept up the attack by asking what increase in the military establishment would be required if the United States should take over as a "receiver" or "trustee" all the German colonies. Borah asked Knox the leading question whether the United States would have to use troops to keep order in the Cameroons and East Africa. Knox replied "certainly," for force was the only means of ruling "uncivilized countries." He saw a plot not only to have the United States conduct operations in the German colonies and "take them over under a trusteeship or receivership" but also to place the burden of the maintenance of the world upon the United States. He thus clearly linked articles 22 and 10. He believed that such responsibilities could not be assumed without prior consultation with the two Houses of Congress, their appropriate com-

---

[13]Allied and American contingents had been sent to Murmansk, Archangel, and Vladivostok in the hope of restoring bourgeois control, to rebuild the eastern front against Germany and to keep from the Germans or Bolsheviks war supplies at Murmansk. Danger of friction between American and Japanese troops had resulted.—A. W. Griswold gives a brief account in *The Far Eastern Policy of the United States* (New York, 1938), pp. 226 ff.

[14]*Congressional Record,* 65th Cong., 3rd sess., pp. 2353-2355.

mittees and the people of the United States. Vardaman (Democrat, Mississippi) joined in with the rhetorical question whether there was even a "remote possibility" that the Senate would be so "neglectful" of the interests of the American people as to approve such a treaty. But Knox rejoined that it "was the wildest kind of guessing as to what the Senate will do."

Lodge then charged that all these questions had nothing to do with making peace with Germany. He repeated the accusation that the United States was apparently "being involved in some sort of guaranty, either with force or without force, to take care of the German possessions in Africa and the Pacific Ocean." Lodge, the author of the Magdalena Bay Resolution, approved August 2, 1912,[15] was thus one of the first to direct specific attention to the islands which were later mandated to Japan and which today are being demanded by many American admirals. But Lodge declared he did not think "the safety of the world" or the making of peace "is concerned very much with what happens in Africa and in New Guinea and in the Marshall Islands and in the Caroline Islands" since the United States had Guam. Thomas agreed that making peace was the primary concern but that nonetheless one of the most indespensable elements was the disposition of the German colonies. Lodge retorted that he had repeatedly stated that they should be taken from Germany. The Principal Allied and Associated Powers could then turn them over to the Boers of South Africa and the Australians who had captured them, under suitable guaranties. (Lodge was unaware of or indifferent to the "white supremacy" practices of the Beors and other South Africans.) But, he inquired, if the United States should hand them over to a league not yet in existence, why should she be involved in guaranteeing them for

[15]Great agitation had swept over the United States when the news leaked out in 1911 that a Japanese company had been negotiating with a syndicate in the United States for a lease of a large tract of land in the vicinity of Magdalena Bay in Lower California. It would have been an admirable location for a naval base to intercept communications between the Pacific Coast of the United States and the Panama Canal. Lodge's resolution, frequently referred to as his corollary to the Monroe Doctrine, declared in substance that the United States disapproved the transfer of strategic spots in the Americas to non-American private companies which might be in fact agents for a foreign power. The resolution, which had only declaratory significance, was approved by the Senate by a vote of 51 to 4. —*Congressional Record,* 62nd Congress, 2nd sess., pp. 10,045-10,047.

an indefinite future? Thomas pressed his question as to whether the colonies should be "arbitrarily" handed over to the nations that had conquered them. Lodge replied that the *only* concern of the United States was to see that they were not returned to Germany. Perhaps Lodge was right in a general way, Thomas conceded, but nevertheless the question of Kiau-Chow, for example, vitally affected the peace. Lodge pointed out that he had not mentioned Kiau-Chow. Thomas then made clear that he was not in sympathy with the plan for administering the colonies as he understood it, but he did think that their disposition was one of the "vital" elements in the making of peace with Germany. Lodge rejoined that he thought that the "wild tribes" inhabiting the colonies should be under some one's control since he believed they could not form a government. Thomas fully agreed with him. Lodge repeated his feeling that some of the colonies should be placed under South Africa but he did object to "launching out on an indefinite guaranty, we do not know exactly what, which involves eternal meddling in the affairs of Africa." Johnson of California warned that there would be one vote in the Senate that would never be cast for sending American troops to take care of Turkey in Asia or German colonies in Africa.

Walsh reminded the Senate that the discussion had been precipiated by Knox's question as to what increase would be needed in the military establishment if the United States should undertake as the mandatory of the League supervision of all the German colonies. Walsh could not conceive that the American delegation would try to impose any such burden upon the United States. But even if there were no cause for alarm, he would like to point out that the cost of military establishments in African colonies was not high since the rank and file were Native troops. He mentioned this fact not in order to win support for the idea that the United States should become the "mandatary" [*sic*] over the German colonies. But it was evident that the problem was not so simple as Lodge had made it appear. Handing over the German colonies to the Union of South Africa would probably be unsatisfactory to France, Belgium or Portugal. But if the American delegation accepted such a burden, it was because it could not escape it. After further discussion Lodge feared that it was "one [of those problems] that should be decided without involving us in more negro problems." (He was probably recalling the failure of his Force Bill which had sought to give Federal protection to Negro voters in the South.)

Lewis did not wish any one to think that Wilson would allow the inhabitants of the territories to be hurled "into some community lap as one would throw peas and potatoes in a market basket to be thereafter carted away and distributed to such beneficiaries as may bid for them." Such a procedure, he added, would violate the president's basic principle of self-determination. He believed that when the truth was known, they would find that these inhabitants had been temporarily transferred "to the concentrated order or combination of nations called a league . . . until there shall come the opportunity to make such disposition as their permanent welfare would disclose as necessary." He could not believe that the United States had pledged herself to any permanent disposition of these peoples without giving them a chance to express their wishes on the subject. He suggested that the German navy be turned over to the league to do the job of policing, thereby avoiding the "militarism of either blacks in Africa or whites in America or in any other country." Kirby (Democrat, Arkansas) wanted to know whether the United States had spent more than thirty billion dollars and suffered 263,000 casualties in order to give the South African possessions to England, Alsace-Lorraine to France. Rather surprisingly, it remained for this Southern Democrat to sound the apparently most humanitarian note.

> If we should withdraw from the peace conference [he declared] without establishing some kind of league of nations that will gaurantee in some sort of effective way peace to the world and fair treatment to the weak and small and subject peoples of the earth and protection from exploitation by the strong and powerful, we may have done a disservice to mankind instead of a benefit in helping to vanquish the central powers.

But it may be surmised that Kirby was defending Wilson rather than the subject peoples. Moses (Republican irreconcilable,

New Hampshire) linked the subject with the Monroe Doctrine when he declared: "If we take possession of the German colonies and undertake to administer them and become mandatory for them, we have in that very hour—I do not care whether there is any declaration to that effect or not—abandoned the Monroe Doctrine." For if the United States insisted upon meddling in European affairs, she could not deny European nations the right to interfere in the Western Hemisphere.[16]

This discussion of January 30 and 31 constituted the most extended debate up to this time dealing specifically with the mandating of the German colonies. The most significant aspect of it is that only one Democrat, Kirby, made any real plea in support of the system and that plea sounded almost anemic in the face of the attacks made upon it by Republicans and other Democrats. Ransdell (Democrat, Louisiana) later inserted on February 25 an editorial from the *New Orleans Item* that opposed the assumption by the United States of responsibility for Turkey and Africa and "backward" peoples in other parts of the world but favored such assumption for weak and small nations.[17]

By February 26 senators were in possession of the exact terms of the mandate article, number 19 as it was then designated. Cummins asserted that it surpassed article 10 "in its repugnance to good morals and to the civilization of the world." It was not only bad in itself but the "grossest violation" of the Constitution he had ever seen. Under it the United States could be forced to accept a mandate for Turkey. The United States, he argued, had a right to acquire by conquest or purchase territory that was destined either for admission as a state or to be governed directly as a territory. (Cummins was cutting the cloth to suit himself.[18]) But there was nothing in the Constitution, he continued, that permitted the United States to act as tutor,

[16]*Ibid.,* 65th Cong., 3rd sess., pp. 2419-2425.

[17]*Ibid.,* 65th Cong., 3rd sess., p. 4208.

[18]Practically all lawyers and historians would agree with the statement of Charles A. Beard that the "founders of the American system . . . did provide, of course, for territorial government, but they viewed territories as potential states held only in temporary tutelage." —*American Government and Politics* (5th ed., New York, 1928), p. 430.

especially since she would have to prepare the territory for independence. If he ever heard of a lawyer who argued that the United States could surrender sovereignty over territory to a league, he would tear up his certificate to practise law. He repeated the refrain that acceptance of the mandate would require an army of over 100,000 men who would have to be sent 5,000 miles from home, an even larger number of civilian employees and the expenditure of more than a billion dollars. He would prefer to disarm the Turks just as Germany ought to be disarmed and then allow them to work out their own destiny.[19] He did not estimate the number of troops or the cost of accepting a mandate over Africa since, in all probability, such an eventuality never entered his mind.

Owen contended that the British and French colonies were in effect "republics" but that the German colonies had to be protected and safeguarded by some form of administration that would establish and maintain peace and good order, internal and external. Article 22 provided a "reasonable and just method for administering the affairs of subject peoples and developing them into democracies." He insisted that the consent of the dependent peoples was recognized. (He was in error as far as the inhabitants of the German colonies were concerned.) He suggested that the article might be amended to provide that the bill of rights of civilized states, as far as applicable, should be recognized as part of the principle of government of backward peoples. Thus Cummins who opposed the treaty as it stood bitterly denounced the mandate system and Owen, the Southern Democrat who favored the treaty, supported it. For the same reason, probably, Owen also denied that there was any likelihood that the proposed International Labor Organization would interfere in the domestic affairs of the United States.[20] But whatever Owen's reasons may have been, he seems to have been more sincere in advocating the mandate system than any other senator except France.

Senator France (Republican irreconcilable, Maryland), a

[19] *Congressional Record,* 65th Cong., 3rd sess., pp. 4309-4316.
[20] *Ibid.,* 65th Cong., 3rd sess., pp. 4320-4322.

native born Southerner, announced on the same day, February 26, his support of the league if it was to help uplift the backward and exploited peoples of the world. Although Owen cited the loyalty of Britain's colonies during the war as evidence that she had tried to give justice to her colonies, France insisted that to try was not enough. "Justice must be accomplished," he declared. "The same heathenism, the same savagery, exist today in the heart of Africa as existed when the pyramids were new. . . . The liberals of the world today demand results, and they will have them." There were many nations which still had reactionary governments that looked with suspicion upon any effort to advance and improve the conditions of backward peoples. Owen agreed, adding: "This is not altogether untrue of the United States."[21]

On the evening of this same day Wilson, who had returned from Paris, had a conference at the White House with the Senate Committee on Foreign Relations and the House Committee on Foreign Affairs. Unfortunately, no stenographic report was made of this conference as of that on August 19, 1919. Indeed, the varying explanations as to what took place on February 26 probably suggested the necessity for the later stenographic report. Hitchcock in denouncing the *New York Sun's* account of the meeting mentioned Ireland, immigration, American participation in European wars, but he made no mention of the mandate system.[22]

Lodge made the opening attack on the full text of the Covenant on February 28. In a speech that on the whole was temperate he declared that he hated war and decried partisanship. He wanted only a careful study of the document. He criticized article 19 as he did many others because it contained an argument and a statement of existing conditions. Article 10 would constitute a guaranty by the United States of the colonial territories in Africa as well as territory elsewhere. Although article 19 was one of the "great" articles, "oddly enough . . . it

[21] *Ibid.*, 65th Cong., 3rd sess., p. 4325.

[22] The *Sun* stated February 27, p. 2, that "most of the guests left the presence dazed in mind." The article was headlined: "Mandatories Voluntary." See also *ibid.*, February 28, pp. 1-2, March 1, pp. 1-2.

did not state who was to select the mandatories; nor was it clear whether a mandatory was bound to accept it." He would not discuss the general question of the right of the United States to hold territory in tutelage since Cummins had done so. The one thing to do was to make peace with Germany and bring the "boys" home.[23]

Later in the same day Lenroot (Republican, Wisconsin) went further than had Lodge and suggested an addition to article 19 that was later embodied in one of the reservations. He first criticized the article because it provided for consulting the inhabitants of the Turkish communities but not those of the German colonies. Like many others he was probably less interested in assuring these latter self-determination than he was in attacking the covenant. He also criticized the article because it provided for the compulsory acceptance of a mandate. Since Turkey would surely select the United States as mandatory because America's motives were not suspect, he argued, the article should be amended so as to make acceptance optional and then only with the consent of the legislative body of the nation involved. And finally, the nation should be permitted to surrender the mandate to the league at any time.[24] This last suggestion was not later placed in the reservation, perhaps because there was no likelihood that Congress would accept a mandate.

Knox on March 1 made a much more devastating attack upon the Covenant than had Lodge or Lenroot. Searchingly criticizing each article, he condemned article 19 because of the vagueness of the language as to the organization and operations of the permanent commission and as to the manner of selecting the mandatory. He voiced the same criticism that Lenroot had made about the violation of the principle of self-determination in the German colonies. But most important of all, he felt, was the fact that whoever selected the mandatory American boys could be sent to the "arid regions of Armenia or to the sleeping-death regions of central Africa, or to the wildernesses of south-

[23] *Congressional Record,* 65th Cong., 3rd sess., pp. 4520-4528.
[24] *Ibid.,* 65th Cong., 3rd sess., pp. 4569-4572.

west Africa, or to the inhospitable South Pacific Isles, and when they get there it will be somebody else besides ourselves who will determine how long they shall remain, by what laws they shall govern the people, and what shall be their measure and rules of protection." Some other authority would also determine how many billions of dollars would be wrung by taxation from the American people to spend in the territory over which the United States had been made mandatory perhaps against the wishes of the American people. All these provisions would violate those clauses in the Constitution that give Congress the power to raise and equip armies, raise revenues and make appropriations and that give the president the power to control and direct the operations of the army in the field, including the power to lay down the rules which shall operate and control between the occupying army and the inhabitants of the territory occupied. Like Lodge he wanted to have the peace treaty signed, to leave the league to the future, and to bring the boys home as soon as possible.

Hardwick (Democrat, Georgia, who had been defeated by an administration supporter in the November elections) gave the usual arguments of the Republican opposition and repeated in slightly different words Knox's criticisms of article 19. He quoted the statement from Wells already cited by Knox and declared that Wilson would "find a pretty sweet time" trying to get support for such a proposal "anywhere in the South or the West when the people understand that one of the questions remitted to the league of nations is to consider and redress the so-called wrongs and grievances of negroes in the South and of Japanese and other orientals in the West."[25]

A bit of twisting the lion's tail was enjoyed by Sherman on March 3. The Illinois irreconcilable was participating in a filibuster in order to have called a special session which would permit the opposition the more effectively to build up its case because of Wilson's absence. He charged that article 19 unloaded the guardianship of the British Empire upon the United

[25] *Ibid.*, 65th Cong., 3rd sess., pp. 4700-4703.

States. "This article smells loudly of professors," he devastatingly sneered, since it sounded like a lecture on ethnology blended with an appeal to subscribe largely to foreign missions. He alleged that Wilson's "cryptic generalities" in asking for $750,000,000 for the expansion of the navy were really for the purpose of making the United States "the trustee of modern civilization." He also lugubriously pictured American boys dying all over the world.

In the session that began at 10:30 P. M., March 3, Lodge introduced the famous round-robin signed by thirty-seven Republican members and members-elect of the 66th Congress urging that a treaty of peace be signed with Germany and that after that had been done the proposal for a league of nations should be taken up for "careful and serious consideration." Since Swanson (Democrat, Virginia) objected, the resolution could not be given immediate consideration. At two o'clock in the morning La Follette demanded a special session to pass important legislation and to advise the president on the treaty. France, in supporting the proposal (and in killing time) queried: "How shall the governments meet their responsibilities to the people of Africa, for example?" Many of its inhabitants, he again declared, were living under conditions of "heathenism and savagery substantially the same as those which prevailed in the unknown Hinterland when the Pyramids were new and the great Rameses ruled in Egypt." Was the African question to be solved by new partitions and conflicts, all for the purpose of exploitation, or should there be cooperation for development of the peoples with due regard for their environments and their needs? "The whitening bones and rusting manacles which strew the paths from Central Africa to the Portuguese slave colonies on the west will plead to Heaven in protest until this African problem is solved in some constructive and humanitarian way," he concluded in support of the suggestion of the special session.[26] Rarely have the halls of the Senate resounded with such an eloquent plea in behalf of the

[26]*Ibid.*, 65th Cong., 3rd sess., pp. 4864-4869, 4967-5003.

African Natives as in this filibuster by a Southerner, a Republican from Maryland, an irreconcilable who later demanded that a reservation in behalf of these Natives be added to a treaty that he was pledged to defeat with or without reservations.

The filibuster succeeded in preventing the passage of necessary legislation but it did not win a vote for a special session. At noon on March 4 the Senate adjourned *sine die*.[27] Wilson, who had been waiting in his room at the Capitol, declared that it was "not in the interest of the right conduct of public affairs that I should call the Congress in special session while it is impossble for me to be in Washington, because of a more pressing duty elsewhere, to cooperate with the Houses." In order to offset the effect of the round-robin, Wilson prevailed on Republican ex-President Taft to speak with him at the Metropolitan Opera House that same evening. It was in this speech that Wilson promised to bring back a treaty with the Covenant so closely intertwined that "you cannot dissect the covenant from the treaty without destroying the whole vital structure."[28] The fact that the mandates article was so inextricably interwoven with the rest of the treaty was one of the already manifest principal reasons for the opposition of the third session of the 65th Congress to the Covenant and to the Treaty. Perhaps for that reason Wilson mentioned only the Austro-Hungarian Empire and the Turkish Empire when he referred to the victors as "the trustees of the assets of those great nations."

---

[27] *Ibid.*, 65th Cong., 3rd sess., p. 5021.
[28] *New York Times*, March 5, 1919, pp. 1-2.

Chapter IV

THE NOVEMBER, 1919, REJECTION OF THE TREATY OF VERSAILLES

When the absolute need to pass appropriations before the end of the fiscal year, June 30, compelled Wilson to call a special session which opened May 19, 1919,[1] the president and his supporters believed that the opposition could be defeated. The threat embodied in the round-robin of thirty-seven members of the 66th Congress, more than enough to constitute the one-third plus one who could defeat the treaty, caused sincere friends of the treaty to make determined efforts to assure ratification. Acting upon the strong insistence of Hitchcock, of leading Republicans like Taft, ex-Secretary of State Root, President Lowell of Harvard, and other prominent members of both parties, Wilson had obtained changes in the Covenant which they had urged. These included a specific reference to the Monroe Doctrine by name (article 21); a direct statement that domestic questions should be excluded from the League's jurisdiction (article 15, paragraph 8); withdrawal from the League (article 1, paragraph 3); voluntary acceptance of a mandate (article 22, paragraph 2).[2]

But the growing support for the treaty led Lodge and his supporters to plan more vigorously their *modus operandi.* They were greatly aided, of course, by the fact that the Republicans now controlled the Senate and therefore the strategically important Committee on Foreign Relations. By that time Lodge, the new chairman of the Committee, had decided that "there was only one thing to do and that was to proceed in the discus-

---

[1]Wilson was quite superstitious, believing for example that the number thirteen was lucky for him. On that account he had dropped the Thomas from his name so that Woodrow Wilson made thirteen letters. Wilson might well have considered nineteen his unlucky number. This crucial session opened on May 19, 1919; the White House Conference of August 19 did him no good; the first rejection of the treaty occurred on November 19 and the final one on March 19.

[2]There are good summaries in Fleming, *United States and the League,* 153 ff., and in Holt, *Treaties Defeated by the Senate,* pp. 266 ff., Schriftgiesser, *Lodge,* pp. 331 ff.

sion of the treaty by way of amendment and reservation." During the ensuing delay a letter from Root insisting on reservations to eliminate article 10, to make more certain the right of withdrawal from the league, to protect further domestic questions and the Monroe Doctrine, gave joy to the strong reservationists and to the irreconcilables. Lodge further stalled for time by having the entire treaty of several hundred pages read aloud line by line, thereby consuming two weeks. The Committee held public hearings—another six weeks—the first time in the history of the United States. The Senate considered the treaty in open executive session which gave the gallery *claque* an opportunity to demonstrate its attitude. Finally, it should be remembered that amendments could be inserted or reservations added by a simple majority whereas a two-thirds majority was needed on the resolution of ratification.[3]

Sherman lost no time in making a general attack upon the Covenant. On May 23 he specifically denounced obligatory acceptance by the United States of mandates in Africa and Asia. He asserted that a million soldiers would be required to fulfill the responsibilities and duties of the United States in foreign lands. He insisted that the voluntary acceptance of the tutelage of colonies and backward areas would be no defense against the assumption of the burden by the United States since the league was the president's creation and the other eight members of the Council would be justified in expecting the United States to assume this burden.[4]

Reed in what Holt appropriately describes as "worthy of a stump speech in South Carolina in the 1890's"[5] contended on May 26 that none of the "grave objections" in the original document had been removed. He then launched upon his most protracted and emotional diatribe against the "colored league of nations." The seventeen "dark countries" were "so low in civilization that they constitute the very dregs of ignorance. . . . They are the victims of superstition and are steeped in barbar-

[3]See the references in the preceding footnote.
[4]*Congressional Record,* 66th Cong., 1st sess., pp. 170-171.
[5]*Treaties Defeated by the Senate,* note 88, pp. 291-292.

ism." The people of Liberia and Haiti in particular were "baby murderers, . . . creatures of the forest who sacrifice their children to idols." Reed, of course, offered no proof for the extreme statements that he made. Hitchock in reply to a question from Reed said that if Britain and France had no objection to the admission of Haiti and Liberia who were "being financed by the Unted States, and largely controlled by the United States," the United States would not suffer very much from their membership in the League. Reed shifted his position so frequently, objecting now because the United States would be outvoted especially by the British Commonwealth and again because a unanimous vote would be required, that he was forced to admit that he condemned any league. Reed then went on to call attention to an article in the *Crisis*, the organ of the National Association for the Advancement of Colored People, which had declared that a league of nations was absolutely necessary for the " 'salvation' " of Negroes. "Chew on that quid in your reflective moments, you men of the South!" he admonished. He then appealed to the prejudices of West Coast senators by discussing the attempt of the Japanese to introduce a racial equality clause into the Covenant. He closed his speech by disclaiming any prejudice against colored races.[6]

By contrast to the vituperative attacks of men like Reed, the supporters of the Covenant were at best only lukewarm in advocating the humanitarian aspects of the treaty. Robinson (Democrat, Arkansas) listed the transfer of the German colonies as one of the guaranties of her future "harmlessness" and pointed out that some agency was necessary to govern them. Not once did he express any interest in or sympathy for the inhabitants of the mandated areas. He pointed out that in article 22 the acceptance of the mandate was entirely optional and referred to the treaties of the United States with New Granada, Panama and Haiti as evidences of her willingness to accept responsibilities outside her territories. (He did not point out the corresponding benefits to the United States.) He weakly answered Reed's diatribe by saying that "to exclude a nation be-

[6]*Congressional Record,* 66th Cong., 1st sess., pp. 235-246.

cause it is small or backward would be to counteract the very influences which the league itself is intended to promote," and that there was no race question involved in the establishment of the league.[7]

Hiram Johnson was not particularly interested in the mandate system, reserving his siege guns for article 10 which had increasingly become the target of opponents of the league. On June 2 in a long, previously announced speech, he stated that he was unable to take up the "important" question of mandates. But he warned in closing: "This league means that American boys shall police the world; . . . that Europe, Asia and Africa may draw upon us in their every dispute and quarrel." Nor did Borah at first show interest in the mandates. On June 5, for example, he was concerned lest the league be dominated by Great Britain when her interests were involved, because Britain dominated Reed's seventeen small nations. This statement gave Reed an opportunity to go into his act again. Williams, four days later, condemned Reed for his "stupid" appeal to race prejudice but he quickly gave the assurance that "there is not a man in the United States that will respond more quickly than I to an appeal to race supremacy, race integrity, race purity and to making this country a white man's country." He recognized at the same time the right of brown and black races to secure their racial supremacy in their respective countries.[8]

Walsh of Montana, the Liberal and constitutional authority, was primarily interested in the constitutional aspects of the mandate system. He inquired on June 11: "If full governmental authority may be exercised for all time over newly acquired territory consistently with the Constitution, how can it be doubted that a limited authority may be exercised for a limited time over regions not now a part of our possessions?"[9]

Knox was, of course, opposed to article 22 just as to the Covenant as a whole. He introduced a resolution stating that the Senate would look with disfavor upon all treaty provisions that went beyond the aims for which the United States had

[7] *Ibid.*, 66th Cong., 1st sess., pp. 328-343.
[8] *Ibid.*, 66th Cong., 1st sess., pp. 501-509, 693-705, 795.
[9] *Ibid.*, 66th Cong., 1st sess., pp. 955-963.

gone to war. On June 17 he explained that his resolution did not call for a vote either for or against the League and did not attempt to make the League a party issue. But six months had passed and Europe was still in chaos. His speech which covered about ten pages of the *Record* did not mention the mandates. Neither McCumber on June 18 nor Thomas on the next day mentioned the colonial problem. Sheppard (Democrat, Texas) on June 20 denied that the Covenant would compel the United States to administer the affairs of other lands in any way "contrary to our will." It was not imperative, he pointed out, that any nations should accept a mandate. But he made no extended remarks on the point. Sherman on the same day contended that the League would be dominated by Catholic nations. Ashurst (Democrat, Arizona), who accused Sherman of being "foggy and windy at the same time," declared that the opposition was constantly shifting ground. Reed had pictured the League as being dominated now by kings and monarchs, then by the British Empire and next by Negroes. The spectre of Bolshevik Russia had been paraded across the Senate floor and now the ghost of Papal supremacy. Ashurst later quoted from an article by George Sylvester Viereck in the current issue of *The American Monthly* (formerly *The Fatherland*) stating that the new Germany would not consent to economic or political tutelage and predicting that the confiscation of her ships and colonies and one-sided disarmament would lead to a rebirth of militarism. Borah in his speech of June 25 mentioned Shantung, Poland, Ireland, Egypt, but not the former German colonies or Turkish possessions. Nor did Wilson's long cablegram of June 28, the day the treaty was signed, which contained a long sentence on the mandates provoke any debate. (Gerry (Democrat, Rhode Island) made a long speech in support of the League in which he discussed each article but he merely summarized article 22. Fall (Republican irreconcilable, New Mexico) and Spencer (Republican, Missouri) did not mention it.[10]

[10] *Ibid.*, 66th Cong., 1st sess., pp. 1216-1222, 1264-1276, 1372-1374, 1431-1450, 1737-1749, 1952-1953, 2054-2064.

The president laid the treaty before the Senate on July 10. Although he did not give a complete summary of it, he explained that in addition to the settlement of the European frontiers there had been established the system of trusteeship. He believed that none of the compromises in the Covenant "cut to the heart of any principle." Swanson made the opening speech in support of the treaty on July 14. His discussion of the mandate principle was primarily an encomium of American administration in Hawaii, the Philippines and Puerto Rico (!). Article 22, a "most commendable feature," would "enable America, where independence sprang from resistance to colonial wrongs, to restrain in the future the hand of colonial oppression. America, the first and staunchest friend of colonial rights, will have her sphere of usefulness enlarged."[11] He did not refer to the third-class Negroes[12] in his own state of Virginia.

Poindexter the next day had inserted an article by the Republican Publicity Association that attacked the mandates provision because, it alleged, it would give Britain which already controlled one-quarter of the land surface control over four-fifths of the captured German colonies The article further inquired why a portion of the Turkish territory should be selected for administration by the United States as mandatory. If the United States had to be a mandatory, she should rather select a portion of the former German colonies. This was one of the very few instances in which the Republicans made even a left-handed suggestion that the United States accept a mandate over any part of the former German colonies.[13] But, as previously pointed out, senators frequently inserted statements that supported their position without implying that they subscribed to everything in the statement. There is no other evidence that the Washington irreconciliable wanted the United States to accept this obligation.

Norris (Republican irreconcilable, Nebraska) reiterated on July 15 the principle of no-transfer of a people without their

---

[11] *Ibid.*, 66th Cong., 1st sess., pp. 2336-2339, 2533-2540.

[12] This term has only recently come into current usage. See *What the Negro Wants* (Chapel Hill, 1944), edited by the author.

[13] *Congressional Record*, 66th Cong., 1st sess., p. 2587.

consent but he did not apply it to the former German colonies. He was, however, much distressed by the brutalities inflicted upon the Koreans by the Japanese and by the British support for the Japanese claims against China. These latter, he asserted, were for the purpose of facilitating the acquisition by the British Commonwealth of the former German possessions in the Pacific south of the equator. Underwood (Democrat, Alabama) referred to the struggles for empire as one of the principal causes of war but he looked to article 10 rather than to article 22 as providing the remedy.[14]

Africa, along with Europe and Asia, interested Colt (Republican, Rhode Island) on July 17, primarily because of the fact that the enforcement of terms of peace concerning them prevented the divorcement of the Covenant from the treaty. King again advocated the assumption of the mandate over South-West Africa by the Union of South Africa. He asserted that Britain had earnestly urged the United States to accept the mandate, but that sentiment in this country was opposed to acceptance. Since the atrocious administration by the Germans required transfer, and since Britain "magnanimously" did not desire South-West Africa for herself, there was no one left but the Union to take it. The Anglophobe Sherman opposed any mandate for the United States and denounced Britain who had always found it expedient to "maintain the blessings of English civilization" in lands where diamonds and gold had been discovered. Britain's dream of a Cape-to-Cairo railroad could now be realized, he argued. He further contended that when Britain got the former German colonies in East Africa and got article 10 by which the United States would undertake to preserve territorial integrity around the world, Britain would be obtaining "a substantial share of the practical worldly loaves and fishes in this treaty." Borah inquired how, under the treaty, the Egyptians, Chinese, Irish, Indians or Koreans could get their independence but he did not ask what guaranties there were that the inhabitants of the mandated areas would receive

[14] *Ibid.*, 66th Cong., 1st sess., pp. 2593-2597, 2600-2602.

theirs. An interesting article by Frederick C. Coudert, a well-known New York lawyer, inserted at the request of Williams, presaged in some respects the regionalism proposed in this present era. Coudert thought that "an extension of the very valuable plan for mandatory control would meet the objection [of sending American troops to fight in Europe's war] as far as it has any foundation, by dividing the world into four zones, one of which would be the Western Hemisphere, in which the United States could intervene when anarchic or other conditions threatened world peace." '[15]

Neither Pomerene (Democrat, Ohio) nor Harrison (Democrat, Mississippi) mentioned the mandates on July 21. Harrison did rebut the charges that Great Britain, colored peoples or the Pope would control the League. At no time, he stated, had Negroes ever been able to dominate whites. In his state Negroes outnumbered whites, but the white people were "practically unanimous" in support of the League. (By implication the views of the Negroes, if any, did not matter.) McNary (Republican, Oregon), Johnson (Democrat, North Dakota) and Beckham (Democrat, Kentucky) also supported the League on July 22 without mentioning the mandates. Moses referred briefly to the loss of Germany's overseas possessions. McKellar on the next day supported the Covenant, derided Reed's color scare and mentioned briefly the mandate system, pointing out that the United States did not have to accept a mandate. An article in the *Los Angeles Times* of July 14, inserted at the request of Williams, asked how the mandatory powers could be entrusted to certain nations if there were no association to see that their powers were not abused. Four editorials in the *National Republican*, inserted at the request of Sherman, attacked the "rotten borough" Democratic states and asked why the Democrats reserved democracy for the export trade alone.[16]

Japan's claims to Shantung were cited by Lenroot on July 24 as an example of the flagrant violation of Wilson's Fifth Point. He further contended that since the United States was one of

---

[15]*Ibid.*, 66th Cong., 1st sess., pp. 2720-2735, 2820-2822.
[16]*Ibid.*, 66th Cong., 1st session., pp. 2927-2946, 2983-3000, 3018-30023, 3043-3049.

the Principal Allied and Associated Powers, she would become "the owner of an undivided one-fifth of all of Germany's colonies." He was gratified that the compulsory acceptance of a mandate had now been removed. He had no objection to the article as it then read, but he believed it would be "wise to give notice to the other members of the league, by accompanying resolution, but as no part of the ratification, that Congress will alone exercise this discretion and that the Executive has no power to do so." Fletcher (Democrat, Florida) immediately challenged Lenroot's assertion that the United States would have an undivided fifth interest since the former German colonies had been assigned to mandatories. Pittman (Democrat, Nevada) on the next day pointed out that if negotiations were reopened, Japan would be sure to try again to have her racial equality clause adopted.[17]

The sacred right of revolution proclaimed in the Declaration of Independence was preserved by article 10, according to Walsh of Montana on July 28. He made no application of the sacred right to the mandated areas. Gay (Democrat, Louisiana) on the following day declared that the League made "suitable provisions" for the League to guide backward peoples "to the pathway of self-government." Like most of the others who supported the League, he displayed no great enthusiasm for the idea. Thomas praised England's colonial administration and quoted from an article in *Harper's* that forecast high protective tariffs and governmental support in the marketing of goods in "secondary states, protecotrates, and colonies." One of the twenty-three reasons listed by Ransdell on July 31 in support of the League was the argument that "it would place under international control all investments and concessions in backward nations." (This statement could not be entirely justified by the language of article 22.) As for the welfare of the Native inhabitants the Louisiana senator was silent. Owen, who announced that he would support the Covenant with or without amendment or reservation, contended that although the United

[17]*Ibid.*, 66th Cong., 1st sess., pp. 3090-3100, 3130-3135.

States had intervened under the Monroe Doctrine in Haiti for the principles stipulated in article 22, there was no danger that a foreign nation would try to exercise the rights of mandatory in the Western Hemisphere. Owen did not include among his eighteen reasons for supporting the League the preparation of backward peoples for self-government, but he did praise the provisions intended to promote the better interests of the worker.[18]

King on August 1 stated that it would be improper to talk of an American mandate over Constantinople and Armenia until after the treaty had been ratified. Even then there would probably be "great opposition." Fall referred sarcastically to speeches that reminded Americans of their "duty" to the "Buddhists of Japan and India, the Confucians of China, the Voodoo worshipers of Africa, the fire worshipers of Persia, the Mohammedans of Turkey, the Jews and Gentiles of the world." The League possessed sovereignty over the Saar, the Rhineland, and the German colonies, he asserted. He charged specifically that the "vague provisions" of article 22 gave the Council "direct control and supervision" over the mandated areas.[19] The language does not permit this interpretation.

The disposition of colonies and the selection and jurisdiction of mandatories, along with arbitration of disputes, the delay of three months after an award before going to war, and the reduction of armaments might all have been agreed to by the American people, declared Sterling (Republican, South Dakota) on August 4. But the American people were not ready to guarantee the peace of the world and back the guaranty by making war upon every nation charged with being an aggressor. This guaranty, he enumerated, extended to all the British Empire, the French Congo, Sierra Leone, Algeria and the Italian possessions in Africa. The next day Newberry (Republican, Michigan, who was forced to resign on November 22 after having been convicted of violation of the Federal Corrupt Practices Act) inserted on behalf of his colleague, Townsend, an

[18] *Ibid.*, 66th Cong., 1st sess., pp. 3222-3229, 3313-3320, 3398-3410.
[19] *Ibid.*, 66th Cong., 1st sess., pp. 3476, 3483-3484, 3492-3499.

article the keynote of which was " 'Democracy is not yet safe for the world.' " It declared that most of the hundreds of millions of people who had been deprived of " 'the steadying force of regularly constituted government were unfit for self-government.' " They were, however, entitled to the opportunity to develop it, " 'perhaps under mandatory power and direction.' " Watson (Republican, Indiana) made a long speech about Japanese interests in China. Brandegee (Republican irreconcilable, Connecticut) on August 5 inserted a long article by William George Jordan, a prolific writer on many subjects, which analyzed " 'Forty-one Points of Vagueness, Danger, Ambiguity, Impracticability and Weakness of the Covenant of the League.' " Article 22 received most elaborate treatment. He pointed out that the wishes of the inhabitants of the former German colonies would not be consulted in the selection of the mandatory. He condemned the power of the " 'nine men of Geneva' " in terms similar to those later used in deriding the "nine old men of the Supreme Court." He charged that the mandatories were to force " 'an unwilling civilization and an alien code of morals and ethics on peoples to whom the whole thing may be repulsive.' " Who would pay the expenses of administering the mandates, he inquired. He portrayed the United States as a " 'Don Quixote, setting forth on a glorious mission to redeem the world.' "[20]

Provisions for mandates "in relation to the freedom in transit and equitable treatment of commerce," along with articles 8, 10, 11, were enumerated by Kellogg on August 7 as among those cited by the opposition. Turkey, which had received increasing attention in August, was discussed on the next day by Thomas and McCormick (Republican irreconcilable, Illinois, who had succeeded Lewis). McCormick inquired why the United States should be asked to assume control over Constantinople when Greece was there to assume the burden. Thomas replied that since Constantinople was a cosmopolitan city and was desired by many European nations, none of them could

[20] *Ibid.*, 66th Cong., 1st sess., pp. 3607-3611, 3619-3623, 3633-3645, 3670-3680.

be delegated the task. The reason for the choice of the United States was, according to Thomas, therefore obvious.[21]

Lodge, in a previously announced speech—his first since the treaty had been laid before the Senate—voiced on August 12 his well known objections to the League. He wanted to limit strictly the "interference" of the United States in the affairs of Europe and Africa, but the United States must guard her interests in the Pacific. Williams in his reply referred to the fact that this advocate of a hands-off policy had "fathered the Force bill against the southern white people." The main question, according to the Mississippi senator, was not whether articles 10, 11, 22 or others should be amended but whether the senators approved or disapproved the treaty as a whole. He ridiculed the idea that half the world would combine against the United States to compel her to admit Japanese immigrants. He had "started to say" Negroes from the West Indies who were "infinitely less desirable citizens than the Japanese," but Negroes were already being admitted. "You boys up North" did not want to keep out these West Indians for fear of losing the Negro vote. Hitchcock recalled that Lodge had advocated a league at Union College in 1915. Borah defended Lodge by stating that great men change their minds. Reed on August 13 inserted an article from the *St. Louis Post-Dispatch* which favored the usual reservations plus one that would " 'remove all obligations upon us to oppose the right of peoples to change their form of government or to secure their independence as did the American Colonies from England.' " Williams inserted an article by the well-known war correspondent, Frederick Palmer, that assured there was no danger that the United States would be called upon to accept a mandate for Armenia because European nations would not tolerate American soldiers " 'in this domain of European interests.' " American mandates would be on her own continent, as in Mexico for example.[22]

Among the half of the world's population protesting against the treaty, declared Borah on August 18, were the 33,000,000

[21]*Ibid.*, 66th Cong., 1st sess., pp. 3680-3692, 3712-3713.
[22]*Ibid.*, 66th Cong., 1st sess., pp. 3778-3789, 3816-3819, 3911-3912.

additional subjects acquired by Britain under the treaty. (The senator must have obtained his information from the same source as that from which he learned in 1939 that there was not going to be a war.) The right of revolution of "backward nations under a mandatory" would have been denied under a resolution introduced by Owen on August 20.[23]

The mandate question loomed large in the conference between Wilson and the Committee on Foreign Relations at the White House on August 19. The president read a prepared statement urging early consideration of the treaty. He was frankly unable to understand why doubts should be entertained about certain articles in the Covenant. He reminded the Committees he had returned to Paris and secured acceptance for the four points desired, namely, express recognition of the Monroe Doctrine, no authority for the League to act in domestic matters, the right of withdrawal, and the safeguarding of the constitutional right of Congress to determine all questions of peace and war. Lodge, after discussing the steps in the drafting of the Covenant and the participation of the United States in reparations, came to the question of the former German colonies. But his own interest lay in the possibility for the United States to acquire one of the Pacific islands for naval purposes. After a discussion of Shantung, Yap and the secret treaties, Fall stated that he had been curious to know who would defend the mandated areas against external aggression. The president replied: "Primarily, the mandatory power." The colloquy continued:

"Senator Fall. The mandatory power would have that character of sovereignty over the possession which would compel it as a duty to defend the mandate province?

"The President. Yes.

"Senator Fall. Then a qualified sovereignty would in that instance, at any rate, compel the mandatory of the league first to defend the colony.

"The President. I should put it this way, Senator: We had

---

[23] *Ibid.*, 66th Cong., 1st sess., pp. 3934-3936, 4012.

in mind throughout the whole discussion of the mandate idea the analogy of trustees. The States taking those under mandates would be in the nature of trustees, and of course it is part of the trustee's duty to preserve intact the trust estate? [*sic*]"

"Senator Fall. But out of the funds of the trust estate?

"The President. Oh, yes."

Fall said that he would not pursue that question further for the time being. The discussion returned to Shantung and then Johnson of California asked whether the pending treaties with Austria, Hungary, Bulgaria and the Ottoman Empire did not all possibly deal with the subject of mandates too. The president, giving perhaps unwittingly the opposition another stick with which to belabor him, agreed that these treaties would "no doubt create certain territories which fall under the trusteeship which will lead to mandatories." Johnson rejoined that evidently a very important part of the world settlement remained to be made. They discussed the secret treaties of which, Wilson insisted, he had had no knowledge prior to the peace conference,[24] and the British Empire (which Wilson called a "diplomatic unit") from which the dominions would be excluded in the event of a dispute between the United States and England. New then asked: "What agreement, written or verbal, has been entered into by the American delegates touching the assignment to various States of mandatories [*sic*] under the provisions of article 22?" The conversation continued as follows:

"The President. None whatever.[25]

"Senator New. If it be understood that Great Britain or her dominions will act as mandatories of the territory in Africa lately held by Germany, what advantage of a practical nature is expected to accrue, and whom will it benefit, from subjecting the British or dominion administration to the mandatories of such nations as Liberia, Italy, or any others?

"The President. Mandatories of Liberia?

---

[24]For a recent discussion of Wilson's prior knowledge see the review of H. F. C. Bell's *Woodrow Wilson and the People* (New York, 1945) by Gerald W. Johnson in *New York Times Book Review,* June 10, 1945, p. 3.

[25]See above, p. 4.

"Senator New. Yes.

"The President. I do not understand, Senator. The whole system of mandates is intended for the development and protection of the territories to which they apply—that is to say, to protect their inhabitants, to assist their development under the operation of the opinion of the world, and to lead to their ultimate *independent existence*."

One is forced to conclude that New either did not understand the mandate system or that he was deliberately misrepresenting it for the purpose of harassing the president. But one also wonders why Wilson did not press further his advantage resulting from New's confusion. At all events, it is highly significant in view of later controversies over the eventual objective of the mandate system and in view of the discussions at San Francisco over independence or self-government to note Wilson's unequivocal statement that the ultimate goal of the mandate system was independence.

Moses then gave it as his understanding that the United States became possessed "in fee simple of an undivided fifth part" of the former German colonies. Wilson replied: "Only as one of five trustees, Senator. There is no thought in mind of sovereignty." Moses then attacked from a different angle by inquiring: "Such possession as we acquire by means of that cession would have to be disposed of by Congressional action?" The president responded that he had no thought at all on that subject, no plan or recommendation to make to Congress. He was waiting until the treaty had been disposed of. (Wilson could have had in mind only the Turkish territories because, as already indicated, the distribution of the German colones had already been agreed upon.)

Lodge then called attention to the fact that the conference had lasted about three hours and a half and that it was a half hour past lunch time. The president invited the Committee to have lunch with him.[26]

One of the most interesting observations about this part of the conversation is the fact that none of Wilson's supporters

[26]*Conrgessional Record*, 66th Cong., 1st sess., pp. 4013-4031. Italics not in the original

joined in it. Perhaps they considered it as one of the points on which they would not go down fighting. It seems to me also that Wilson was not at his best in these exchanges.[27] Was he already fatigued? Was he seeking to keep the good-will of the opposition? Had he lost some of his fervor for article 22? The answer to the last question would seem to be in the negative when one has read the comments he made about it in his tour around a large part of the nation in September.

Poindexter during the discussion on August 20 of the stenographic report of this conference argued that the League would decide what mandate would be given to the United States. But Pittman flatly rejected this interpretation, insisting that the president realized that a mandate could not be forced upon any nation. Poindexter rejoined that the stenographic report showed the president as having said that the League would determine the mandatory. Pittman maintained that Poindexter's interpretation was incorrect, as indeed it was. But Poindexter continued with the admonition that it would be very interesting to know whether it was intended that an edict of the League could make the United States mandatory for Constantinople or Armenia. Pittman retorted that only persons who opposed the treaty could place any such interpretation upon it.[28] At all events it is evident that again it was the Armenian mandate that gave most concern to the senators.

McCormick later in the day again portrayed Britain's alleged completion of the "'all-red'" route from Cape to Cairo and also the "'all-red'" route from Cairo to Calcutta by control over Persia. The debates on article 10, he declared, had made abundantly clear that the protection provided in it made the United States "guarantors of all the frontiers of the world, including those of the far-flung autocracies of France and Britain." He gave a lurid review of the perfidy and aggression which had been the basis of empire in Africa and Asia and

---

[27]Fleming, on the other hand, considering the conference as a whole, contends that Wilson had proved himself more than a match for his critics.—*United States and the League*, p. 316.

[28]*Congressional Record,* 66th Cong., 1st sess., p. 4037.

painted the usual gory picture of the bleached bones of American "boys" in various parts of the world. "In the high places of Asia, the snow will cover the frozen bodies of Americans perhaps now unborn, and American mothers—little girls today, mayhap, playing in the summer air about the dooryards—will mourn their sons fallen in the desert wastes of Syria and Egypt."[29] This seems as appropriate a place as any to point up the obvious fact that American "boys" have died in many places that the opponents of the League never mentioned although the United States did not join it. But the effect of these speeches must have been tremendous because in 1944 a member of a church in Mount Pleasant, Washington, asked me whether my plea for American interest in dependent areas would entail keeping large numbers of American troops abroad for an indefinite period.

The International Labor Organization which, in recent years has inspired more confidence among many persons interested in dependent areas than has the Permanent Mandates Commission, was condemned by Thomas on August 22. He could see nothing it could do that would "yield an equal and coincident benefit to the United States, where labor conditions are generally superior to those of any other class." This was also true, he contended, as far as Britain and her dominions were concerned.[30]

The question of the character of the title received by the United States to any part of the German overseas possession had been the subject of written questions left by Fall with the president at the White House conference. Wilson replied that article 119 simply vested in the Principal Allied and Associated Powers " 'a trusteeship with respect of their final disposition and government.' " His reply to a second question stated: " 'There has been a provisional agreement as to the disposition of these overseas possessions, whose confirmation is dependent upon the approval of the league of nations, and the United States is a party to that provisional agreement.' " This com-

[29] *Ibid.*, 66th Cong., 1st sess., pp. 4041-4044.
[30] *Ibid.*, 66th Cong., 1st sess., p. 4154.

munication from the president was printed without reading and was not followed by any discussion.[31]

Neither Nugent (Democrat, Idaho) nor Fall on August 27 mentioned the subject. Williams on the next day revealed no real sympathy for the mandate system. He broke off the reading of an article from the *New York Times*, dated August 25, which accused the Committee on Foreign Relations of having " 'invited the discontent of Europe, Asia and Africa to come and be heard,' " to say that

> Certain American colored people have been before the committee this morning to argue the right of savage tribes in Africa to self-determination, and all that sort of thing; tribes that nobody contends to be anything but wild savages with breechclouts about them.

He went on to say, however, that "there was more justification for hearing those American people concerning those of their race in Africa, in Togoland, and elsewhere than there was in hearing a great many others appearing before the committee."[32]

Whether Townsend was referring to the inhabitants of mandated areas is unclear from his statement of the same day. He wanted the United States "to make the meaningful statement that inasmuch as it is receiving nothing from Europe, Asia, Africa, and believes in representative democracy and self-determination of peoples, it can not and will not assist in forcibly transferring peoples and their territory to other governments, and to agree to maintain these enlarged boundaries perpetually against external aggression." If he was including the mandated areas, he was arguing against article 10 rather than against article 22.[33]

In discussing the harsh terms imposed upon Germany, Knox on August 29 alleged that the United States had become a "tenant in common" with the British Empire, France, Italy(!) and Japan of Germany's former colonies. Like Lodge he feared potential trouble if some powers other than the United States obtained possession of the Pacific islands. Hitler could have cited Knox's later assertion that not only did Germany receive

---

[31] *Ibid.*, 66th Cong., 1st sess., pp. 5024-5031.
[32] *Ibid.*, 66th Cong., 1st sess., pp. 4259-4265, 4404-4407, 4408-4415, 4451-4452.
[33] *Ibid.*, 66th Cong., 1st sess., pp. 4453-4455.

no credit for the territory ceded, but she also lost "the efforts of a generation to provide an outlet for her rapidly increasing surplus population, which now must and will find expanding room elsewhere." The more Knox considered the treaty, the more he was convinced that the United States should not be a party to it at all.[34]

Owen, on the other hand, apparently came out in favor of article 22 when on August 30 he stated that he favored "the liberty and freedom of all peoples sufficiently advanced to govern themselves or under the mandatories where backward and not yet qualified."[35]

Since Williams rarely spoke in favor of article 22, it is pertinent to examine an editorial from the *Baltimore Sun* which he considered a complete answer to Knox. Among the "beneficial" aspects of the Covenant, stated the *Sun*, it " 'makes colonial governments responsible to a tribunal composed of representatives of all the civilized nations of the world.' "[36]

Irishmen and their sympathisers had great delight in denouncing Great Britain for acquiring new territory and for not granting Ireland "home rule," but they displayed little interest in self-determination or self-government for the inhabitants of the mandated areas. The Negro delegation, referred to by Williams, had consisted of William Monroe Trotter of Boston and seven others. Trotter, speaking for the National Equal Rights League, asked that a "racial equality" clause be added to article 23. J. T. Thomas of Cleveland wanted the United States to become the mandatory for the Cameroons in order "to open a new world for the educated American Negro, under the direction of trained white American statesmen, soldiers and diplomats." Eventually, he asserted, American commerce would reign supreme in Africa. The Reverend W. H. Jernagin of Washington, speaking for the National Race Congress of America, urged that the Natives of Africa be permitted to participate in their own government as rapidly as their develop-

[34] *Ibid.*, 66th Cong., 1st sess., pp. 4493-4501.
[35] *Ibid.*, 66th Cong., 1st sess., pp. 4547-4551.
[36] *Ibid.*, 66th Cong., 1st sess., pp. 4601-4602.

ment warranted. Charles William Sumner of Indianapolis, on behalf of the International Association for the Freedom of Africans, also wanted the United States to accept the mandate for the German colonies in Africa, especially to save the Natives from the Union of South Africa.[37] Apparently the Committee listened as courteously as it did to other delegations.

"Even the liberation of Africans and others from German colonial oppression" was one of the guaranties of the permanent removal of the German menace, Hitchcock declared on September 3 after the Committee's vote of nine to eight to adopt amendments had destroyed in his opinion American participation in the League. Likewise in criticizing Knox's proposal that the United States "scuttle and run," he again made a plea for the treaty rather than for protecting subject peoples. Borah on September 5 mentioned Egyptians, Indians, the Balkan peoples, the Irish and the Koreans among the 900,000,000 who would be "subject peoples" if the League was adopted. He read from an article in the *New York Tribune* of the same date the suggestion that the United States send 200,000 troops to Armenia as quickly as possible in order to substantiate his argument. When Norris on September 5 mentioned briefly the principle of no-transfer without the consent of those traded, he made no application of the principle.[38]

In September Wilson began a tour that took him to the West Coast in an effort to build up public sentiment in favor of the treaty. Although his speeches, in which he covered the most important aspects of the Covenant including frequent valuable references to article 22, were periodically inserted in the *Record*,[39] they rarely provoked interesting discussion. Lodge on September 8 introduced a compilation of extracts from the writings of Jefferson in opposition to foreign alliances and interference in European affairs in order to offset the arguments advanced by Wilson in Columbus, Ohio, St. Louis and Kansas

[37] Sen. Doc. 106, 66th Cong., 1st sess., pp. 757-903, 679-698; *Congressional Record*, 66th Cong., 1st sess., pp. 4611-4619, 4659-4718.
[38] *Congressional Record*, 66th Cong., 1st sess., pp. 4726-4731.
[39] *Ibid.*, 66th Cong., 1st sess., pp. 4997-5010, 5585-5595, 5937-5951, 6236-6255, 6403-6424.

City, Missouri. McCormick inserted extracts from Wilson's messages and addresses which, he asserted, showed Wilson's inconsistencies especially with respect to self-determination. Among these extracts was a portion of the cable that Wilson had sent to Russia, May 26, 1917, stating that " 'no people must be forced under sovereignty under which it does not wish to live. No territory must change hands except for the purpose of securing those who inhabit it a fair chance of life and liberty.' "[40] McCormick probably no more applied this principle to the inhabitants of the German colonies than Wilson had done when he sent the cable to Russia.

Poindexter in attacking Wilson's tour singled out the president's suggestion that the United States protect Armenia. He made the usual speech about the American soldiers who would have to be sent to Europe, Asia, and Africa in performance of responsibilities incumbent upon the United States if she joined the League.[41]

But Wilson's tour had so alarmed the opposition that several irreconcilables, notably Borah and Johnson, began to trail him and Lodge on September 10 laid his committee's report before the Senate in open executive session. One of the forty-five amendments advocated by the majority report needed to be considered at once, he declared, because an attempt was being made in Paris to force upon the United States the control of Armenia, Anatolia and Constantinople "through the medium of a large American army." Four reservations dealt with the familiar subjects of withdrawal, article 10, domestic jurisdiction and the Monroe Doctrine. The reservation on article 10 also covered the mandates. Although, Lodge explained, the Covenant provided that the acceptance of a mandate was voluntary, article 22 did not specify who in any country had the right to accept or refuse it. The decision as to accepting a mandate must rest "exclusively within the control of the Congress of the United States as the reservation provides and must not be delegated by

[40] *Ibid.*, 66th Cong., 1st sess., pp. 5010-5011, 5018-5024.
[41] *Ibid.*, 66th Cong., 1st sess., pp. 5024-5031.

inference, to any personal agent or to any delegate or commissioner," he insisted.[42]

Hitchcock announced on behalf of the minority members of the Committee that he hoped to file a minority report the next day. Kenyon (Republican, Iowa), observing that no one else wanted to discuss Lodge's report, pulled out all the stops. He would not support the Covenant without reservations even if every man, woman and child in Iowa did. He made no reference to the reservation on mandates.[43] Hitchcock's report, presented on September 11, urged ratification without amendment or reservation, deplored the policy of delay of the majority[44] and emphasized the resulting industrial and commercial instability. The amendments had no merit, he insisted, and adoption would be equivalent to rejection. The reservations were in actual fact alterations and were drawn for the express purpose of destroying the League and defeating the treaty.[45]

The views of Harding who ran for president in 1920 on an ambiguous League plank naturally arouse interest. He asserted that the imperial powers "wanted annexations and extensions and creations, and they wanted this Republic, with its resources . . . to guarantee the changes they had wrought." But he mentioned only Armenia among the proposed mandates. He was not indifferent to the "cruelties of barbarity" but "measureless as our resources are, large as our man power is, and chivalrous as our purposes may be, we are not strong enough to assume sponsorship for all the oppressed of the world." He proclaimed his intention to vote for the Committee's amendments and reservations.[46]

Williams in his reply, hardly a masterpiece, inserted an article from the *New York World* of the same day which had called Lodge's report " 'Prussian' " and one from the *New York Times* which had declared that " 'All is lost, if these reck-

[42] *Ibid.*, 66th Cong., 1st sess., pp. 5112-5139.
[43] *Ibid.*, 66th Cong., 1st sess., pp. 5139, 5149-5155.
[44] For Lodge's explanation of the delay see *ibid.*, 66th Cong., 1st sess., p. 5112.
[45] *Ibid.*, 66th Cong., 1st sess., pp. 5213-5215.
[46] *Ibid.*, 66th Cong., 1st sess., pp. 5219-5225.

less men of the Foreign Relations Committee have their way.' "[47]

On September 15 Sherman inserted an editorial from the *New York American* of the same date which stated that if the League were " 'properly toasted and shredded, there is no reason why it should not be universally used as a breakfast cereal, and boiled in milk it would be an invaluable food for infants.' " McCumber on the same day presented an individual report as a member of the Committee which inquired why the same code of morals that governed individuals could not govern nations. This moral code, he charged, had been ignored in the majority report. His own reservations made no reference to article 22.[48]

Later in the day consideration of the report was begun. Jones (Democrat, New Mexico) analyzed each article in detail, briefly pointing out that the United States could not become a mandatory without her consent. Overman (Democrat, North Carolina) who also favored ratification made no mention of mandates. Calder (Republican, New York) did not discuss the mandate reservation but he inserted an article which declared that the League was not only " 'a shame of stagnation, but . . . a contrivance of subjugation' " since under article 22 the peoples of the greater part of Africa were forbidden to bear arms, build fortifications, establish naval bases, or practise military training. Sherman in a lengthy speech made his usual attack on Britain and asserted that the United States was "undertaking to become the guardians of all the failed [*sic*] nations in the world." He cited only the Shantung agreement as violating Wilson's no-transfer principle. He repeated the rumor that Wilson sought to impose on the United States a mandate over Armenia and accused the banks and insurance companies of having organized a campaign in support of the treaty since Europe and Asia offered them an immense field for profit.[49]

Lodge in a long speech on September 16 defended his shift from the days when he favored a league and quoted from an

[47]*Ibid.*, 66th Cong., 1st sess., pp. 5232-5236.
[48]*Ibid.*, 66th Cong., 1st sess., pp. 5353-5354, 5356-5359.
[49]*Ibid.*, 66th Cong., 1st sess., pp. 5390-5400, 5488-5490, 5491-5501.

editorial dictated by Theodore Roosevelt which had urged the United States not to become " 'an international Meddlesome Mattie.' " Since Roosevelt had not seen before his death the details of the League, the ex-president had naturally not been able to discuss them with Lodge, but the latter felt that he and Roosevelt were in complete agreement. He quoted a number of statements by Wilson which he said were not entirely consistent. Williams defended Wilson and, in accordance with his usual practice, inserted an editorial from the *New York Journal of Commerce* of September 12 which declared that the reservations were unnecessary, but he did not mention mandates. The reading of the entire text of the treaty with the changes suggested by Lodge's Committee was then begun. Lodge refused to make any promises as to when he would call up the first amendment for consideration.[50]

Wadsworth (Republican, New York) and Nelson (Republican, Minnesota) on September 19 and Thomas on the next day did not refer to the mandates. Reed on September 22 made another vituperative attack on Wilson, repeated his diatribe about the seventeen dark countries and added a long list of colonies which could be made self-governing in a few days' time by their respective countries, thereby increasing the domination of the darker races. But he barely mentioned article 22. He did insert an article which attacked any acceptance of a mandate by the United States for Armenia and Syria. Rather inconsistently Reed also inserted an article that criticized article 22 because " 'it annihilates the dream of future freedom for peoples under dominion of world powers.' "[51]

The battle of articles continued on September 24 when Cummins inserted one from the *New York American* of September 7, 1919, portraying American boys dying in far distant lands and Williams inserted one which declared that one of the reasons why the United States went to war was to help " 'the little peoples of the earth.' " Fletcher inserted a statement adopted by the Brooklyn League of Nations which declared that there

[50] *Ibid.*, 66th Cong., 1st sess., pp. 5501-5515.
[51] *Ibid.*, 66th Cong., 1st sess., pp. 5618-5625, 5700-5723.

was no need for the mandate reservation on article 10 since under the plain language of article 22 mandates could be conferred only upon those nations that accepted them.[52]

During the executive session of September 24 Frelinghuysen (Republican, New Jersey) attacked the mandate system by quoting from statements made in the House of Commons on July 21, 1919 by Lt. Col. Hilder and H. W. Bottomley. The former contended that the outstanding feature of the treaty was the fact that it put the British Empire at the highest point it had ever reached with respect to territory and world influence. Bottomley complimented the prime minister on his great acumen in securing Britain as the mandatory for some of the ex-German colonies because " 'before we get on very far with the ex-German colonies the league of nations will come to an untimely end, as every experiment of that kind has done.' " (Bottomley's prediction is especially significant in the light of the discussions at San Francisco concerning the disposition of these mandates of the League that failed.) Frelinghuysen added the usual grim spectre of American boys dying in Armenia and other places. The next day New repeated this argument.[53]

On September 26 Cummins insisted that it was nonsense to contend that the United States had gone to war to make the world safe for democracy. She had gone to war to whip Germany and her duty in making peace was thereby limited. Wilson should have said that the United States, " '3,000 miles across the sea, will not become the arbiter or policeman for Europe, Asia, or Africa.' " Cummins referred to his own speech of February 26 when he had objected to the League's issuing a mandate requiring the United States to administer the affairs of a foreign country. That objection had been partially met. If the reservation requiring approval by Congress were approved, the objection would be fully met because he could not conceive that Congress would be "so unmindful of its constitutional limitations and so indifferent to the welfare of the people

[52] *Ibid.*, 66th Cong., 1st sess., pp. 5821-5824.
[53] *Ibid.*, 66th Cong., 1st sess., pp. 5841-5849, 5899-5902.

of the United States as to enter upon any such insane undertaking." He likewise denounced the obligation in the form of men and money that would devolve upon the United States in keeping "these restless, warring, half-civilized people in peace with each other." He, therefore, wanted article 10 completely eliminated. Owen vouchsafed that he had no fear of the "negro bugaboo" as far as the question of domestic jurisdiction was concerned. As for the six votes for the British Commonwealth he stated that Cuba, Haiti, El Salvador, Honduras, Nicaragua and Panama would probably vote with the United States. Brandegee added the usual slur about Hedjaz, Liberia and Haiti. Williams pointed out the consequences of amending the treaty.[54]

Lynchings and other acts of lawlessness in the United States gave Borah an opportunity to warn that American institutions at home were being destroyed and that embarking upon the ark of the Covenant would complete the process. The United States would lose her individuality and we would "all become one happy family—American, Japanese, Chinese and Hottentot." Williams in replying to Borah attempted to justify the lynching of a "miserable black beast." He then inserted a poem in support of the League, "Are We Our Brothers' Keepers?" Borah categorically declared that "there can be no justification for the lynching of any human being" and returned to the charge that under the League the United States would have to furnish aid in protecting the British Empire. Edge (Republican, New Jersey) did not discuss mandates. Fall queried whether the United States was going to accept the Constantinople mandate, take over Turkey and send her sons "to guard Turkish harems." American labor, he asserted, needed no help from the other labor of the world. He called attention to the clause in the treaty requiring that Germany return "to somebody in South America [*sic*] the skull of some old nigger."[55] Like Borah he believed that it was better to look after problems at home and to "sublet the job of looking after the labor of the

---

[54]*Ibid.*, 66th Cong., 1st sess., pp. 5952-5967, 5981.

[55]The skull in question was that of the Sultan Mkwawa in East Africa.

world." He wanted the words "and Associated Powers" taken out of articles 118 and 119 in order to prevent the United States from being one of the recipients of the German colonies and he would refuse to allow the United States to become a mandatory. He would not become a party to a "farce" by which the United States would enter into an agreement for the governing of the former German African colonies when the British and French flags were already flying over them by agreement on Wilson's part. Thomas demanded proof that Wilson had agreed to any division of the former German colonies. Fall cited Wilson's reply that there had been a provisional agreement to which the United States was a party. Knox repeated the question about the acquisition by the United States of an undivided fifth part. The question had therefore occurred to him: "How can the property of the United States and the sovereignty of the United States be conveyed away in advance by any agreement to which Congress is not a party?" Fall, of course, proclaimed his inability to answer the question. Moses, however, reminded the Senate that Wilson had spoken of the United States as "trustees" of the undivided fifth part. Fall contended that the United States had the same rights in this one-fifth as in the Philippines. But even Knox corrected him by reminding that Wilson had told him (Knox) that "he would certainly hope that the United States would take nothing." Knox added that he fully agreed with that view and Fall stated that he was in accord with it. He recalled, however, Wilson's statement that it would be the duty of the mandatory to protect the mandated areas. Moses interjected that there was no point in trying to straighten out the president's "contradictions since the United States was asked to accept the treaty as an act of faith." Fall agreed with Moses that not even the American delegation in Paris could correctly interpret the treaty except those parts which they had helped to draft. Fall then contributed this muddy conclusion:

> If the United States is to get nothing of the German colonies, as she is not to get anything, and they have already been divided up, Japan having gotten a part, Great Britain a portion, Portugal[!] a part, France

> a part and they are all actively in process of division or have been divided, and the flags of these different nations are flying over them, if there is to be an amendment to the league covenant restricting or in any way reserving the right of the United States Congress to pass upon mandates for any foreign countries, then certainly, logically, we should strike out the provision by which the United States takes an undivided one-fifth interest in property which already has been given away with the acquiescence of the President of the United States.[56]

Williams again resorted to an article, in open executive session on October 1, for an exposition of his attitude. This one, by Charles R. Seymour (later editor of *The Intimate Papers of Colonel House*) in the *Yale Review*, October, 1919, declared that the Fourteen Points had been accepted as the basis of peace by both allies and enemies. Seymour mentioned briefly the colonial problem as one example of the close connection between the treaty and the Covenant. Fall joined battle by inserting an article from the *New York American* by Israel Zangwill which denounced the League and charged that under article 22 each mandatory could administer its mandate as it saw fit. Wolcott (Democrat, Delaware) insisted that article 10 would not prevent the Irish from getting their independence. Although he quoted the reservation on article 10, he did not develop the part devoted to the mandates. He condemned the permission granted to representatives of various racial groups to appear before the Committee and called for an early vote on the treaty.[57]

The Senate as in the Committee of the Whole and in open executive session considered on October 2 a series of amendments introduced by Fall. In reply to a question from Walsh of Montana, Fall stated that he would prefer to place under mandate a *nation* that could not be depended upon to protect its racial and religious minorities. They had been discussing Roumania. On the following day King quoted a prominent labor leader in Britain as having said that part XIII of the treaty would be used to gain rights for Negro laborers in the United States. Thomas refused to accept any such "irresponsi-

---

[56] *Ibid.*, 66th Cong., 1st sess., pp. 6076-6091, 6130-6132, 6133-6143.
[57] *Ibid.*, 66th Cong., 1st sess., pp. 6191-6203.

ble conjectures," but warned that unless the lynching of Mexican laborers stopped, trouble might ensue. King made it clear that he deprecated lawlessness as much as did Thomas, but he did want to know whether the proposed international labor organization would have the right to fix national wages, establish insurance and old-age pensions. If it did, he opposed it.[58]

Senator France in a carefully prepared speech delivered on October 8 and 9 devoted more attention to Africa and other dependent areas than did any other senator. In his preliminary analysis of twenty-five defects of the League he charged that no definite time limit was fixed after which the inhabitants of the mandated areas would be free, that members of the League reserved the right to exclude non-members from trade with the mandated areas, that it was expected that the United States would assume control over Armenia and the most turbulent portions of Europe, thus continuing war. He inserted a manifesto of the British Trade Union Congress and the Labor Party which urged that the training and educating of dependent peoples should be undertaken not only in the mandated areas but in all dependent areas. France denounced English reactionaries for resisting these pleas. But the great rising mass of people throughout the world would bring about the ascendancy of principles which would result in the uplift of mankind. He then castigated the European colonial powers, especially England, for their exploitation of the Natives of Africa, and called upon Americans to "share the white man's burden" in Africa. He believed that American Negroes would willingly share in the great undertaking. As for the Republican Party, the party of Abraham Lincoln, it was pledged to furnishing fair opportunities and the best educational facilities to the colored people of the United States. Although he was a Southerner, he would build for the colored people the best schools and urge the graduates to go to Africa and help their brethren there. In this way perhaps the inscrutable plan of Divine Providence in bringing Negroes from Africa would be understood and achieved. A lengthy exordium portrayed the evolution of "a new, great sis-

---

[58]*Ibid.*, 66th Cong., 1st sess., pp. 6265-6279, 6326-6332.

ter republic, which, with its material achievements and moral triumphs, would surpass the glories of the Golden Age of the ancient Egyptian dynasties."

The next day he again denounced the imperialistic nations, this time especially for their failure to include in the Covenant a general provision for the protection of missionaries. They were allowing only their own missionaries to go into their respective territories because they would promote the exploitation of the subject peoples. Unless the Covenant was amended to conform with the ideals of the United States and the recommendations of the British Labor Party, then the treaty should be rejected and a new world council called.[59]

It is extremely difficult to understand this solicitude of the irreconcilable senator except perhaps in terms of his final plea for rejection. He must have known that his condition precedent for ratification had no chance of adoption. On the other hand, it was not necessary to introduce this particular obstacle, for by this time it must have been evident that the other reservations were not acceptable to Wilson and his followers. France did not need the Negro vote in the Jim Crow state of Maryland. He did not seem to propose the grandiose scheme of sending a million or more Negroes to Africa that Senator Bilbo has frequently urged in recent years as a "solution" to the Negro problem in the United States. Perhaps the senator was sincere.[60]

After Nelson had made a plea for cooperation with the allies in establishing permanent peace, Walsh, Democrat of Massachusetts, a state in which the Irish vote was decisive, charged that the statesmen of Versailles, with the exception of the Americans, applied the doctrine of self-determination to their enemies only. They reserved for themselves the privilege of

[59]*Ibid.*, 66th Cong., 1st sess., pp. 6597-6616.

[60]France was born in Cameron, Clinton County, Missouri, October 11, 1873, but prepared for college at Canandaigua Academy, Canandaigua (near Rochester), New York. He attended liberal Hamilton College (of which Elihu Root is the most distinguished alumnus) in Clinton, New York, from which he was graduated in 1895. He studied at the University of Leipzig on a Root Scholarship and was later graduated from the medical department of Clark University, Worcester, Massachusetts in 1897 and from the College of Physicians and Surgeons, Baltimore, in 1903.—*Biographical Directory of Congress, 1774-1927* (Washington, 1928), p. 985.

repression, subjugation and exploitation. The Shantung provision was "indefensible." He excoriated article 10, the six votes for the British Commonwealth and the dangers to Irish independence. Norris on October 10, 11 and 13, Lodge and others on October 14 discussed many of the familiar topics but not the mandates. Fletcher on October 15 declared that only China could say that Japan had no more right to Shantung than Great Britain and her dominions had to the former German colonies. Owen, pressed by McCumber, admitted that some peoples were not ready to govern themselves. But even the peoples of the Congo, the Oklahoma senator insisted, would some day be capable of governing themselves. However, he developed the principle with special reference to Egypt and incidental reference to China. Shields (Democrat, Tennessee) proclaimed his unwillingness to guarantee the possessions of the British Empire with its six votes. Thomas, Borah, Spencer, Reed, Lenroot and others added nothing of new significance.[61]

Kellogg inquired on October 16 why special protection should be given to labor and not to the farmer. Sherman alluded again to the rumor that 150,000 American soldiers would be needed to administer the Armenian mandate. Johnson of California quoted Wilson's Fifth Point and the relevant principles of February 11, 1918, but he confined their application to Shantung. Williams entered a plea on behalf of Confederate Veterans and the internationalizing of Anglo-Saxon order and liberty. Fall pointed out that the former German colonies had been handed over to the Principal Allied and Associated Powers whereas Shantung had two claimants. Brandegee on October 17 saw in the attempt to interest the United States in Armenia a "composite scheme" embracing Europe, Asia and Africa. Warren (Republican, Wyoming) opposed having the United States become the policeman of the British Empire. Poindexter on the next day discussed Ireland, Britain's six votes, the Monroe Doctrine. Hitchcock accused the opposition of engaging in a filibuster.[62]

---

[61] *Congressional Record,* 66th Cong., 1st sess., pp. 6614-6621, 6872-6890, 6924-6954.
[62] *Ibid.,* 66th Cong., 1st sess., pp. 6989-7014, 7053-7075, 7119.

When the reading of the entire treaty was completed on October 20, Lodge called for a vote on the first amendment. Borah in his attack, October 22, on the six votes for the British Commonwealth charged that the British mandated areas would be included in the British system of preferential tariffs. This constituted proof to him of the "thin and gauzy . . . covering of the true ownership under these so-called mandates." Gronna (Republican irreconcilable, North Dakota) on October 24 apparently made a plea for the independence of all dependent areas when he inquired:

> Must it be said that we are ready or willing to turn over the affairs of government, the principles for which our boys believed they fought, to an executive council composed largely of aliens, and that from now on the several nationalities, many of whom are found among the nations of Europe, and also in Asia and Africa, shall be denied the right of self-determination and must submit to the mandates of this council, regardless of how brutally they may be oppressed or how just their causes for freedom and liberty may be?

It may be surmised, however, that Gronna was really using this plea as another stick with which to belabor the League which, he asserted, would involve the United States in wars in Europe, Asia and Africa. He then took up each article, but instead of discussing article 22 he inserted an editorial from the *Washington Post* of October 20 which commented that the Senate was still in the dark as to the meaning of article 22 because of its " 'ambiguities and hidden meanings.' " The public knew even less than did the Senate. But in the Senate, the article continued, it was believed that as soon as the Covenant had been ratified the United States would have to accept the Armenian mandate. " 'The inevitable tendency of article 22 is to embroil the United States in foreign quarrels,' " the editorial concluded.[63]

Lodge on October 25 declared that he begrudged Britain[64] nothing that she had obtained under the treaty. Sherman two days later, taking time out to berate the "cannibals and voodoo worshipers in the back country of Liberia," charged again that

[63] *Ibid.*, 66th Cong., 1st sess., pp. 7175-7270, 7320-7325, 7418-7429.

[64] Whether Lodge purposely excluded the British dominions in the Pacific is not clear.

Britain might elevate to statehood the former German colonies in Africa, thereby increasing the number of colored nations in the League. La Follette opposed Britain's six votes on October 29. The Wisconsin Liberal opposed article 23 because, he alleged, it would lower the standard of living of the American working man and thereby weaken America's position in the struggle to gain still further advantages for the great masses of labor. Sherman offered an amendment asking the blessing of God on the Covenant. Johnson of California offered one giving the United States equal voting representation with the British Commonwealth in the Council, the Assembly and the I. L. O. His amendment was rejected, 35 yeas, 42 nays. Thomas on October 30 and 31 opposed the labor provisions because they did not permit representation of organized labor. Fernald (Republican, Maine) on November 3 joined in the attack on what Wilson had frequently called during his tour labor's magna carta. He wanted the United States to have forty-eight votes in the League which, he believed, would surely lead the United States into war. Williams inserted a resolution by the Armenian National Union Assembly urging the United States to aid Armenia. Sherman on November 3 and 4 continued the attack on the labor provisions, especially, he explained, after he had seen some of the representatives to the labor conference then meeting in Washington. McCormick also denounced the labor provisions. Gore (Democrat, Oklahoma) made the usual attack on article 10.[65]

After various other amendments had been voted down without discussion of the mandates, Lodge at last on November 6 announced his intention of offering his reservations. After prolonged discussion of voting procedure, fifteen reservations were read. The mandate reservation had now been separated from the reservation on article 10 and as reservation number four read as follows:

> No mandate shall be accepted by the United States under article 22,

---

[65] *Congressional Record*, 66th Cong., 1st sess., pp. 7488-7489, 7556-7558, 7669-7692, 7797-7805, 7867, 7887-7938, 7955.

> Part I, or any other provision of the treaty of peace with Germany, except by action of the Congress of the United States.

Reservation number eight stipulated that no American should serve on any of the treaty commissions, committees, tribunals, courts, councils, or conferences except with the approval of the United States. Reservation number fourteen declared: "The United States declines to accept as trustee in her own right any interest in or responsibility for the government or disposition of the overseas possessions of Germany, her rights and titles to which Germany renounces to the principal allied and associated powers under articles 119 to 127 inclusive." It will be noted that this reservation applied only to the German colonies and not to the Turkish communities but that it included the Pacific islands as well as the African possessions. These reservations along with the others were to be made part of the resolution of ratification which would not become binding until they had been ratified by at least three of the other four Principal Allied and Associated Powers.[66]

During the discussion on November 7 of the first reservation (ratification to be binding when approved by three of the four other Principal Allied and Associated Powers) Smith of Georgia approved reservation number four. King opposed a mandate even with the approval of Congress. But he wondered whether article 22 did not imply the consent of Congress. Smith was not sure, but he wished to be certain before the treaty was ratified. Jones (Washington) insisted that if the United States member of the Council gave his assent, it was binding. Smith agreed with his prompter. Continuing a point which has become a heated issue in 1945, Pomerene wanted to know what provision of the treaty bound the nation by the act of the American member of the Council if he had not been given authority by Congress. Smith had to admit that there was no specific provision to that effect but, he insisted, the "whole spirit" of the Covenant was based upon the idea. When it was borne in mind, he continued, that article 22 was drawn "pri-

---

[66] *Ibid.*, 66th Cong., 1st sess., pp. 8013-8023.

marily" by Smuts, it was understandable why Smuts believed that, as in the Union of South Africa, no parliamentary action was required to approve the acts of the representative. But Pomerene called attention to the clause stating that the "tutelage . . . should be entrusted to advanced nations . . . who are willing to accept it." He did not understand that a member of the Council could any more bind the United States than could an ambassador unless some special legislative authority had been given him. Kellogg asked Pomerene whether under the article as it stood the president or Congress could accept the mandate. Pomerene replied that the law-making power would do so. Kellogg insisted that article 22 did not so specify. Pomerene retorted that no one else had authority to bind the United States. Reed demanded why the specific statement should not be made. Kellogg took the same position. Pomerene insisted that this particular clause needed no more clarification. McCumber reminded Smith that the latter had repeatedly declared that a nation can act only through its legislative body. Walsh of Montana aligned himself with Pomerene and McCumber and added that the action of the Council on which an American member would sit would have to be unanimous in its decisions. He further inquired why the United States should insist any more than should any other signatories upon writing into the Covenant the particular method of giving assent. Smith replied that he wanted an express declaration because he had gathered from a number of places in the Covenant that the representative on the Council was to act for his nation. If senators would read the interview between the president and the Committee on Foreign Relations, they would see that Wilson had suggested that the American representative in Switzerland would of course be in touch with the administration here, so that it could control his actions. But Simth wanted to make assurance doubly sure. He did not want too much power given to a president two years later to dominate affairs through the Council without congressional approval. (Smith obviously feared the possibility that a Republican might be elected in 1920.) Walsh of Montana pointed out that the United States had signed many treaties providing for the appointment of commissioners. Those treaties had not stipulated how the commissioners would be appointed. But Smith still contended that he was opposed to the president's sending commissioners to act under the treaty without submitting their nominations to the Senate. He specifically did not wish to run the risk of any representative in Switzerland, with the approval of the president, "putting a mandate on this country."[67] Thus, in addition to opposition to a mandate under any circumstances there was involved the habitual conflict between the Senate and the president over the control of foreign policy.

Reed tried to get an admission from Smith that the United States had already made a pledge to accept the Armenian mandate. Smith did not know. Walsh of Montana inquired what significance such a pledge would have. Smith replied that it would be tantamount to saying that action by Congress was not necessary to accept a mandate. If the United States accepted the mandate, the most "conservative" estimate spoke in terms of 100,000 soldiers for ten years. McCormick suggested that the cost would be over a billion dollars, a guess which Smith accepted. McCormick then reported the rumor that a "certain distinguished member of the banking house of J. Pierpont Morgan should be made viceroy of Constantinople." Smith had had enough of McCormick's leading questions but he raised the estimate to 250,000 soldiers. Having reached a figure that he apparently believed to be sufficiently alarming, Smith tried his hand at portraying American boys dying of disease "or by the scimitar of the Turks." Yes, he was "intensely" in favor of the reservation. Walsh of Montana still maintained that article 22 needed no further clarification. Lodge's first reservation was agreed to, 48 to 40. The debate on the second reservation did not at first seep over into mandates as that on the first had done.[68]

The right of self-determination formed the basis of a reservation offered by La Follette on November 10. It provided that

---

[67]*Ibid.*, 66th Cong., 1st sess., pp. 8058-8059.
[68]*Ibid.*, 66th Cong., 1st sess., pp. 8060-8139.

> Nothing contained in article 2 of the League covenant or any other provision thereof, shall be construed to deny to the people of Ireland, India, Egypt, Korea, or to any other people living under a government which, as to such people, does not derive its powers from the consent of the governed, the right of revolution or the right to alter or abolish such government and to institute a new government, laying its foundations in such principles and organizing its powers in such form as to them shall seem most likely to effect their safety and happiness.

Another reservation offered by La Follette stipulated:

> The United States hereby gives notice that it will withdraw from the league of nations whenever any member, exercising a mandate or a protectorate over any country, or claiming and exercising a sphere of influence in or over any country, shall without the free and full consent of the people of such country, appropriate the natural resources thereof, or shall, directly or indirectly, aid any individual or corporation alien to such country to acquire any right or title to or any concession in its natural resources, or right or title to its property, real or personal, or shall fail or neglect, within such authority or influence as it may properly exercise, to preserve in trust for the people of such country all right and title to and in its natural resources and real and personal property, or shall fail to exercise such mandate, protectorate, or sphere of influence over such country for the sole benefit of the people thereof.[69]

Again one is left in a quandary as to why an irreconcilable should devote so much thought to the framing of a reservation when he was committed to defeat of the treaty with or without reservations.

Debate on the third reservation (article 10) included a brief mention of Armenia. On November 11, Owen replied to a question by Penrose of the previous day that the Fifth Point was found in article 22. When Norris on the same day asserted that the "prime object" of article 10 was to maintain the world supremacy of the British Empire, he mentioned Egypt, India, Persia but not the mandated areas. Smith of Georgia criticized Wilson for his failure to live up to his promise made in Paris on January 25, 1919, " 'to see that every people in the world shall choose its own masters and govern its own destinies.' " (One wonders how Smith would have applied the principle in his own state.) Reed portrayed a cartoon depicting a muddy Uncle Sam pulling a bedraggled female from a muddy, filthy

[69] *Ibid.*, 66th Cong., 1st sess., pp. 8192-8193.

creek. The woman threw her arms around Uncle Sam's neck and screamed: "'You have saved me; now you have got to marry me.' [Laughter]" The parallel with the treaty was exact, he explained, because the "countries that, according to the theory here, ought to be in the penitentiary and locked up we are establish mandatories [*sic*] over." He maintained the thesis that a "mandatory" was a military occupation. But he referred to only the Armenian mandate which, now, would require a half million or a million soldiers. Owen inserted a resolution of the League for World Federation asking that in accordance with the international contract of November 5, 1918, "'the council should issue to each mandate a charter of liberties and maintain in each an administrative court to ascertain if freedom is being maintaned.'"[70]

Lodge on November 12 persuaded the Senate to lay on the table Htchcock's motion on behalf of sixteen senators asking that debate on the reservations be closed. During the debate on Lodge's third reservation, November 13, La Follette in a long discussion of the spoils of war said that he did not know what portion of the former German Empire France had obtained. On November 15 the Senate voted for cloture.[71]

The scant amount of interest in the mandate reservation is shown by the fact that it was agreed to without debate. But the fourteenth reservation provoked considerable discussion. Townsend felt that the question of mandates had been sufficiently protected. Why, therefore, bind the hands of the United States in the future? "Are we not interested in the Pacific islands formerly owned by Germany?" he inquired. Shields listed the population of the Pacific islands but called attention also to the African mandates. He repeated the statement that the League would eventually disappear leaving Britain in full possession of the mandated areas.[72] The sole question, he continued, was whether the United States was to be trustee for Britain, France, and Italy (!) although no American interest was involved and although the trusteeship might cause the sacrifice of American

---

[70]*Ibid.*, 66th Cong., 1st sess., pp. 8193-8205, 8207, 8216, 8271, 8274-8296.
[71]*Ibid.*, 66th Cong., 1st sess., pp. 8413-8437, 8555-8556.

life and treasure. He therefore favored adoption of the fourteenth reservation.[73]

New, however, with prophetic insight pointed to the strategic importance of the Pacific mandates. He emphasized the fact that the possession of the Marshall Islands "brings Japan more than 2,000 miles nearer to the west end of the Panama Canal than she was without them." If the island of Yap were to go to Japan, then the United States would be deprived of the cable there "or we must go to Japan, hat in the hand, . . . to ask her for the privilege of maintaining a cable station in the Pacific as a relay for our communications with the Philippines." Pressed by Sterling, New asserted:

> The United States, because of her obligations in the Philippines must have for her very own enough of those islands to give her some strategic advantage and not put her under every strategic disadvantage for any emergency that may hereafter arise.

Later in the day Phelan (Democrat, California), after denouncing the secret treaties, prophesied that "the Pacific Ocean is going to be the theater of the great events of the world's future." He praised Seward's foresight in securing Alaska "as a means of defense against any enemy in the Pacific," and referred to a chart which predicted that the white population of California would be submerged by the Japanese in 2010. He was convinced that

> Japan, therefore, is eager to firmly establish herself in the Pacific against that day when the patient and altruistic people of the United States shall, realizing too late their danger, take up arms pursuant to the law of self-preservation.

Phelan also feared that Japan might fortify the islands and not permit the open door in them. He offered a reservation designed to assure to all members of the League the open door in all mandated areas. He stated that he had been advised "by the best naval authorities" that Japan could use the islands not only to attack Hawaii but also the Pacific coast of the United States. Finally, he urged the Senate to reject the fourteenth

---

[72]See above, p. 63.

[73]*Congressional Record,* 66th Cong., 1st sess., pp. 8556, 8617-8619.

reservation since it declared in advance that the United States would take no interest whatever in the disposition of the "mandatory rights." But Shields insisted that the purpose of the fourteenth reservation was precisely to keep Japan from getting the Pacific islands.[74] While it is difficult to follow Shield's reason, it is significant that both opponents and advocates of the fourteenth reservation feared the future use that Japan might make of the Pacific mandates. The jingos were right for once.

Senator France opposed the adoption of the fourteenth reservation because it would finally commit the United States to a policy the results of which had not been carefully considered, while its defeat would leave the United States free to pursue "any policy with respect to this problem, in which we have vital interests, which will serve those interests as well as the cause of world peace and progress." If the reservation were defeated, the question of the final disposition of the former German colonies would be left to the League, with the United States representative participating or not as seemed best. Resuming the theme of his former speech, he declared that adoption of the reservation

> would conclusively prevent our having any large part in the solution of the great problem of the advancement of the peoples of Africa, to which advancement we have already committed ourselves by a national policy long since announced. We would be prevented by the adoption of this reservation from having a voice in the disposition of a question which, if not settled along the lines of broad and unselfish statesmanship, looking toward an open door for all the nations and toward true international co-operation in Africa, contains within it the germs of new wars, and we would be denied the high privilege of working with the other nations for the welfare of those peoples in whom we have a peculiar interest and for whose welfare heavy responsibilities rest upon us. The adoption of this reservation would, indeed, cut the heart out of the league. If we are to be in the league at all, let us not be there voiceless and impotent when this great problem comes up for consideration and discussion.

(I do not know what this "national policy" was. The United States had appropriated $100,000 in 1819 to help found Liberia but had manifested little interest in her ward except when France, Britain or Germany seemed to have designs on it. Else-

---

[74] *Ibid.*, 66th Cong., 1st sess., pp. 8619-8620, 8624-8629.

where in black Africa the United States government had indicated little interest except in the Congo Act and the "Congo Atrocities.") Emphasizing again the importance of the former German colonies in Africa, he mentioned the Belgian acquisition of Ruanda-Urundi. He quoted from the interview between Wilson and the Committee on Foreign Relations the passage relating to mandates, he inserted several newspaper articles dealing with the duties of civilized nations to backward countries and especially with American interests in the Congo. Stanley's discoveries, the senator asserted, had given the United States sovereign rights over the whole region of Central Africa but the United States had not seen fit to exercise those rights. But if the United States should now renounce interest in the more than 1,000,000 square miles of territory that Germany had owned in Africa, the United States should at least reserve the right to say to the League: " 'Whoever may have these colonies, whoever may take this vast territory to administer, must agree to such conditions as we insisted must be applied to the administration of the Belgian Congo.' " He referred to the demand by the British Labor Party in 1917 for the open door in Africa. The time might come, he warned, when the maintenance of the open door in Africa might be most important and when the voice of the United States in African affairs might result in maintaining the peace of the world.[75]

Walsh of Montana, like some other Western senators, was much more interested in the strategic importance of the Pacific islands. But he was "exceedingly averse" to having anything to do with the South African colonies. It had been necessary, however, to adopt a general rule for all the former German colonies. He believed that American interests in the Pacific were sufficiently guarded by article 22.[76]

Reservation fourteen was one of the few Lodge reservations rejected—29 yeas to 64 nays.[77] In the light of American interest in the Pacific today, the discussion and vote are most sig-

---

[75]*Ibid.*, 66th Cong., 1st sess., pp. 8629-8633.
[76]*Ibid.*, 66th Cong., 1st sess., pp. 8633-8634.
[77]*Ibid.*, 66th Cong., 1st sess., p. 8634.

nificant. The discussion was one of the longest after cloture had been invoked. The decisive factor in the vote was probably concern for the Pacific island mandates. But even with this reservation rejected, the Senate failed later to ratify the treaty. After the fifteenth reservation and a reservation by Owen on the British protectorate over Egypt had been rejected, this memorable session of the Senate sitting as a Committee of the Whole in open executive session came to an end.[78]

Debate continued the next day, November 18, on the reservations of individual members. The old arguments about the I. L. O. were rehashed. Reed thought it would be "an anarchist organization." The *Record*, on one of the few occasions that it printed a map, carried one in connection with La Follette's attack on the British spoils in Africa and Asia and British control of the seas. American goods, the Wisconsin irreconcilable charged, would be excluded under the British system of preferential tariffs from the British mandates. (This was theoretically true only with respect to the Class C mandates.) He excoriated British exploitation of subject peoples. The one agency to which Britain could look for the maintenance of the *status quo* was the League. "This covenant," he contended, "closes the door in the face of every people striving for freedom. Not one of the races now held in bondage had a voice in the making of this instrument." But he mentioned only India, Egypt, Ireland and Korea. After quoting Lincoln on the right of self-government, he again denounced Britain.[79]

When various individual reservations had been rejected, France introduced a long reservation that has such historic value that it is quoted *in extenso*. The Maryland irreconcilable's reservation stated:

> Except that, in accordance with the principles declared in article 22, that the tutelage of the peoples which are no longer under the sovereignty of the States which formerly governed them and which are not yet able to stand by themselves should be intrusted to the advanced nations who can best undertake this responsibility, the principal allied and associated powers shall renounce in favor of the United States all their rights and

---

[78]*Ibid.*, 66th Cong., 1st sess., 8634-8644.
[79]*Ibid.*, 66th Cong., 1st sess., pp. 8699-8728.

titles to the colonies and territories in Africa formerly held by Germany and transferred by Germany to said principal allied and associated powers under articles 119 to 127 inclusive and the United States shall act as mandatory of such territories to the end that the inhabitants of these colonies and territories may be civilized, educated, and fitted for self-determination, and to the further end that the United States shall closely cooperate with Great Britain, France, and Belgium and with such other powers as have interests in Africa in a permanent, progressive, and upbuilding policy for the development of all of the peoples and resources of Africa, and further that the ratification of this treaty by the United States shall be only on condition that the principal allied and associated powers take such action as is herein provided by the renunciation of such rights and titles to the United States.

This remarkable reservation, the only formal proposal that the United States assume the mandate over the former German colonies in Africa, received a vote, without debate, which represented the degree of interest of senators and probably of the people of the United States. There were seventy-one nays and three yeas. The names of the three who voted in the affirmative, whatever their reasons may have been, deserve at least to be recorded. They were Ball (Republican, Delaware), France and Sherman, two Republican irreconcilables.[80]

La Follette, in support of his reservations, argued that the mandate article was based upon the assumption that the hundreds of millions(!) of peoples called weak and unable to take care of themselves needed a guardianship. He added: "If this be not a scheme to exploit the weaker nations, to take away from them their coal and their oil and all of their natural resources, for the benefit of those who have the mandates, then you will adopt this reservation. If you are in favor of robbing these peoples—these weaker nations—through mandates, you will vote down the reservation." McCormick stated that he shared La Follette's view as to the character of the mandates but that he could not vote for a reservation that seemed to "dictate the conduct of the members of the league as regards these weaker peoples."

King, however, found fault with La Follette's logic, accusing him of taking the position that when a trustee violated his trust,

[80] *Ibid.*, 66th Cong., 1st sess., p. 8746.

then the cotrustees should flee and leave him free to pursue his perfidy. It seemed to King that it was rather the duty of the cotrustees to remain on watch. La Fallotte countered with the charge that King had voted on one occasion to deprive the United States of an equal vote with Britain, "the one member of the league that is in a position to reap the richest possible results from the mandatory system." La Follette insisted that the other nations badly wanted the United States in the league. They wanted American troops and money. If the United States imposed conditions prior to entering the League, the other members would have to accept them. Reed renewed his attack on the ambiguities and vagueness of the Covenant. The word mandate, he maintained, fell into this category. It was really a euphemsim for "the military occupation of the territory of a conquered people, . . . it bears no relationship whatever to a trust, and when we speak of beneficence in connection with it it is like speaking of the acts of Satan in the gentle language of eulogy."[81]

The reservation was rejected 23 yeas, 51 nays. Ball who had voted for France's reservation voted against La Follette's just as La Follette had voted against France's. France supported La Follette along with Lodge, Knox, Borah, Brandegee, Johnson of California.[82] Again one wonders why these irreconcilables who were determined to defeat the treaty in any form went through the mumbo-jumbo of presenting an apparently well considered reservation. France's reservation, he must have known, had no chance of adoption. Perhaps La Follette believed that his did and that he would thereby make it more difficult for Democrats and mild reservationists to accept the treaty.

After another reservation had been rejected, the Senate was now ready to consider its action as a Committee of the Whole. Hitchcock's amendment to the first reservation was rejected, 36 yeas, 45 nays. Since this vote showed his side doomed to defeat on the other reservations, he proposed that the others be voted

[81] *Ibid.*, 66th Cong., 1st sess., pp. 8752-8753.
[82] *Ibid.*, 66th Cong., 1st sess., p. 8753.

on en bloc. But reservation five had been reserved for a separate vote and Lodge, ever alert, remembered that there had not ben yeas and nays on the fourth reservation. It was carried, 52 yeas to 31 nays. Forty-three Republicans and nine Democrats —Gore, Hitchcock, King, Owen, Reed, Shields, Smith of Georgia, Thomas and Walsh of Massachusetts—voted in the affirmative. All thirty-one negative votes were cast by Democrats.[83]

On November 19 Smith of Georgia declared that he was unwilling to allow Britain to impose the Armenian mandate on the United States. Wilson's letter of November 18 to Hitchcock stating that the resolution of ratification with the Lodge reservations really provided for the nullification of the treaty was read. When the reservations were finally embodied in the treaty, the mandate reservation had become the third. On the resolution to ratify there were 39 yeas and 55 nays with Fall not voting. A second vote on ratification with reservations resulted in 41 yeas and 51 nays. On the first vote four Democrats —Gore, Shields, Smith of Georgia and Walsh ofMassachusetts joined thirty-five Republicans in the affirmative. The thirteen Republican irreconcilables — Borah, Brandegee, Fernald, France, Gronna, Johnson, Knox, La Follette, McCormick, Moses, Norris, Poindexter and Sherman—cast their votes with forty-two Democrats in the negative. On the second vote, three Democrats—Myers, Owen and Pomerene—shifted from the negative to the affirmative, Culberson (Democrat, Texas) and Nelson (Republican, Minnesota) from negative and affirmative respectively to not voting. Fall did not vote on either ballot. On the vote to ratify without reservations, there were 38 yeas and 53 nays. McCumber was the only Republican to vote in the affirmative. Seven Democrats—Gore, Reed, Shields, Smith of Georgia, Thomas, Trammell, and Walsh of Massachusetts—voted in the negative with forty-six Republicans.[84]

This analysis reveals clearly that the Democrats could have obtained at least "a half-loaf" by voting for ratification with

[83] *Ibid.*, 66th Cong., 1st sess., pp. 8754-8755.
[84] *Ibid.*, 66th Congress, 1st sess., pp. 8802-8803.

reservations. There were only three irreconcilable Democrats, Reed, Thomas and Trammell. Their vote added to that of the thirteen irreconcilable Republicans would have been insufficient to defeat ratification. Why, then, did the Democrats defeat the treaty with reservations? In the first place, Wilson had appealed to them on the eve of the vote to cast their vote against ratification with reservations. But in the second place, it has been clearly revealed by this study that the Democrats were only mildly enthusiastic about assuming responsibility for the welfare of dark peoples and for the working man. Even with the mandate reservation there was the danger, however remote, that a Congress might accept a mandate. Similarly, the reservation on the International Labor Organization gave Congress the power to make provision for representation on it. I am not suggesting that this lack of humanitarian zeal was the decisive factor in the failure of the Democrats to support the treaty with reservations. But it was probably a latent facor. The Republicans likewise had no crusading zeal in behalf of the dark peoples or of labor. But the defeat of the treaty must lie at the door of the Democrats.

Chapter V

THE MARCH, 1920, REJECTION OF THE VERSAILLES TREATY

The subsequent debates until the final rejection on March 19, 1920 were really an anti-climax although the second vote showed some significant changes. None, however, revealed such a decisive change as did the vote on the mandates reservation which received the smallest negative vote of any of the reservations.

Yielding to public pressure after the November vote, the mild reservationists had begun to seek some basis of agreement with the Democrats. Such progress was being made among the members of the "Bi-Partisan Conference" which included leaders of the two parties that many friends of the treaty came to feel that passage was assured. But the irreconcilables were as adamant as ever and there is no evidence that Lodge would have yielded to any argument other than a threat on the part of the mild reservationists to leave the party.[1] With every prospect for success in the 1920 presidential campaign, such a drastic action was hardly likely.

Although the Bi-Partisan Conference had failed by the end of January to reach an agreement, the Senate on February 9 agreed to reconsider its vote and sent the treaty back to committee. The next day it was reported out of committee and on February 16 debate was renewed. In the meanwhile, however, discussion had continued on several aspects of the treaty. Hoke Smith of Georgia, who yielded little if anything to any man in his advocacy of white supremacy, made the first attack upon the mandate system. On December 3, two days after the opening

[1]All writers on the subject have relied primarily upon H. Maurice Darling, "Who Kept the United States Out of the League of Nations?," *Canadian Historical Review,* X (1929), 196-211. There is a good account in Fleming, *United States and the League,* chapter XVI, and a short statement in Holt, *Treaties Defeated by the Senate,* pp. 298-299. See also Schriftgiesser, *Lodge,* pp. 348 ff.

of the second session of the 66th Congress,[2] Smith inserted two interviews which he had granted to the *Atlanta Journal.* He had declared: "'OUR BOYS MUST NOT BE DRAFTED to execute mandates or for the wars of the world unless Congress from time to time approves.'" (Once more articles 22 and 10 were clearly linked together.) He quoted H. G. Wells as having said that the League would have to pass upon the treatment of Armenians in Turkey and Negroes in Georgia. (The linking of these two subjects also showed the danger in accepting any mandate.) He had repeated his former assertion that, since the mandates had been largely the handiwork of Smuts, approval by the legislative body in the various countries was not contemplated. He had then devoted considerable space to opposing the Armenian mandate, reiterating the familiar arguments. In his attack upon the I. L. O. he had repeated the appeal that the American standard of living would be lowered if world standards of labor were equalized. McCormick also resorted to an article, this one from *Harper's*, to present his views. The mandate reservation, the article explained, simply made clear the fact that no executive, whoever he might be, could commit the United States to assume jurisdiction over or control by force another country without the assent of Congress. The reservation prohibited nothing and nullified nothing. Lodge on December 13 charged that the labor provisions were an "excrescence" upon the treaty.[3]

Six weeks before the treaty was formally reconsidered King offered a resolution of ratification subject to fifteen reservations. The third differed only slightly from Lodge's mandate reservation, for it declared: "The United States will not accept any mandate under article 22 or any other provision of the treaty, except as Congress may in its discretion determine." His seventh was also similar to Lodge's eighth, stipulating that no

[2]Wilson in his message had made a plea in behalf of labor, adjuring that it "be no longer treated as a commodity," but he said nothing specific about labor in the dependent areas or about the mandates in general.—*Congressional Record,* 66th Cong., 2nd sess., pp. 29-31.

[3]*Ibid.,* 66th Cong., 2nd sess., pp. 62-63, 261-262, 533.

person should be appointed to represent the United States in connection with the execution of the treaty except as Congress provided by law. There was thus substantial agreement between Republicans and Democrats concerning reservations dealing with the mandates. King's thirteenth reservation provided: "The United States withholds assent to article 23, except as the matters are, or hereafter become, the subject of international conventions to which the United States is a party." Again Republicans and Democrats were in substantial agreement. Senator France inserted three days later an article stating that Lloyd George and Smuts wanted the power of the United States to back up England's territorial integrity in all parts of the world.[4]

King on January 8 continued to press for ratification with his reservations. He refused to believe that the vote of November 19 was decisive. He attempted to show how much better the colonial solution was than one proposed by Theodore Roosevelt who had said on September 6, 1918: "'Britain and Japan should keep the colonies they have conquered.'" In praising Wilson's work at Paris, King declared that the president had been opposed to imperialistic policies and to "lust for territorial gains. . . . He endeavored to interpret the hopes and aspirations of the struggling masses and to speak for the submerged and inarticulate peoples not only in Europe but throughout the world." Walsh of Montana inserted an article from the *New Republic* stating that the reservation on article 10 went too far but that the mandate reservation was merely interpretive and should be accepted. On January 31 Lodge got tentative agreement to accept the mandate reservation, now the third,[5] the twelfth and thirteenth reservations. The proposed changes in the other reservations were ordered printed. Reed on February 2 repeated his usual arguments and stated that Bryan had agreed that mandates were contrary to American policy. Hitchcock on February 9, the day the Senate voted to reconsider the treaty, inserted Wilson's letter of January 26, 1919, accepting

---

[4]*Ibid.*, 66th Cong., 2nd sess., pp. 1019, 1214-1217.

[5]Holt for the purpose of convenience makes the mandate reservation the third for both the November and the February votes.—*Treaties Defeated by the Senate,* pp. 295, 297.

Hitchcock's reservations. With respect to the reservation on mandates the president had written Hitchcock from his sick bed:

> I see no objection to a frank statement that the United States can accept a mandate with regard to any territory under article 13, part I, or any other provision of the treaty of peace, only by the direct action of the Congress of the United States.[6]

Although I can offer no explanation as to the reason that led the president to refer specifically to the article providing for the establishment of the I. L. O. rather than to article 22, the association in his mind is worthy of note.

When the Senate in open executive session began on February 16 reconsideration, McCormick immediately raised the curtain. The treaty, he pointed out, affected not only the German people but also "those vast populations in Africa and Asia, new and old subjects of Britain, Japan and France, the three imperial powers." In one of the most intelligent remarks he ever made, he queried:

> If there be any sincerity in the long and unctious [*sic*] provision of the covenant describing the humanizing mission of mandates, why was the league not vested with mandatory power or the supervision over the hundreds of millions already subject to the three great empires as well as over the thousands whose dominions have been freed from the Turk and the Hohenzollern?[7]

Those of us, including notably Dr. Raymond Leslie Buell,[8] who have in recent years advocated the extension of an effective mandate system to all dependent areas could only wish that the Illinois anglophobe had been sincere. The fact that he did not mention also the inhabitants of Belgium, Spain, Portugal and the Netherlands would suggest that he was primarily interested in attacking the three nations that were the principal territorial beneficiaries under the treaty.

Thomas on February 17, in a review of the history of the Fourteen Points and the peace negotiations, declared that the German colonies in Africa and the Pacific aggregated 1,027,620

---

[6]*Congressional Record,* 66th Cong., 2nd sess., pp. 1217-1222, 1358-1361, 2285-2287, 2352-2359, 2622, 2632.

[7]*Ibid.*, 66th Cong., 2nd sess., pp. 2944-2947.

[8]See for example his *Isolated America* (New York, 1940), p. 410.

square miles, about four times the size of Texas, and were "prolific in natural resources."[9] He further stated that he and many others believed that, under the terms of the armistice, these colonies might very properly have been used to compensate some of the allies for the damages inflicted upon them by the war, thus relieving Germany of some of the burden of the indemnity. Such a solution would have been "more than satisfactory" to the countries which had received them. But under the treaty, he correctly added, Germany got absolutely no credit for the cession. Moreover, these colonies owed an aggregate debt of $32,410,000 which was not assumed by the allies. Neither he nor Norris was certain on this point. Challenged, Thomas had to fall back upon J. M. Keynes's *The Economic Consequences of the Peace.*[10]

Senator France on February 20 introduced a joint resolution in which he again demonstrated that he had given more serious consideration to the mandates than had any other senator. It provided for the reestablishment of peace with Germany without annexations and indemnities and the convening of an international conference to deal with international problems. It specifically called upon the president to invite all the signatories of the First Hague Conference and their successors and all other states recognized prior to the sending out of the invitations "to send three delegates each, and also two delegates in behalf of each of the colonies, protectorates and dependencies of the various states having colonies, protectorates or dependencies" to a conference in Washington some time in November, 1920. This conference was to "consult concerning the formation of a more perfect general concert and union, the establishment of the general tranquility, the promotion of the general welfare, and the securing generally of the blessings of liberty to the peoples now living and to their posterity."

The invitations were to be extended with the express understanding that there would be an international conference of the states and an assembly of the colonies, protectorates and depen-

---

[9]For the opposite view see above, p. 3.

[10]*Congressional Record,* 66th Cong., 2nd sess., pp. 2991-2992.

dencies to sit separately but concurrently. All resolutions agreed upon in either body would be purely advisory, and international or "pannational" organs or processes would be purely voluntary. The meeting would be the first of a series which should "establish a system of advisory correspondence, with the continuation committees sitting in the intervals between the conferences to prepare for the international conferences . . . and to carry on the system of correspondence." He then listed twelve specific objjectives of the meetings. The pertinent ones were as follows:

> (c) To formulate a body of international law based on the security of the fundamental rights of the individual as the prime function of all Governments and for applying as between States the analogies of the laws of partnership and cotenancy, and as between States and their respective colonies, protectorates and dependencies the analogies of the laws of conservatorship, guardianship, and trusteeship.
>
> (d) To devise methods for the advancement of the peoples of colonies, protectorates or dependencies from the status of dependencies to that of independence and to full participation in the international conferences.
>
> (e) To promote cooperation among the more advanced nations for the improvement and advancement of the backward territories, particularly those of Africa and parts of Asia, and by the formulation of plans for the reclamation of waste land, for the cultivation of natural resources including water power, for wise colonization, for the promotion of education and the spread of civilization throughout the world.[11]

Although, as will be seen later, this resolution was given no consideration, it deserves analysis. France went beyond McCormick in that he included in his proposal the colonies, protectorates and dependencies of all colonial powers. While he did not specify mandates, it seems impossible in view of his interest in the subject not to include them under the general term dependencies. Not even today is such a proposal given serious consideration. In view of the extended argument at San Francisco over independence or self-government as the ultimate goal, France is again seen as having been far ahead of his generation.[12] That he had given earnest thought to the subject is evident in his concern for the conservation of natural resources.

---

[11] *Ibid.*, 66th Cong., 2nd sess., p. 3161.

[12] I believe that the ideal of independence for all dependent areas is impracticable. Many of them are much too small; the inhabitants of others prefer self-government; if France and the Netherlands were really to carry out their promises of first-class citizenship for all their colonial subjects, no insuperable objection is manifest.

Later on that day Borah discussed Baron Makino's attempt to have a racial equality clause written into the Covenant. "In practice," the Idaho irreconcilable asserted, "equality meant for the white race the abandonment of its standards and tended to destroy the very ideals which had been correctly established."[13]

On February 21 the first reservation (withdrawal) was approved. Because the second reservation (article 10) was likely to arouse much controversy, it was temporarily passed over on February 26. France then had printed without reading his joint resolution of February 20, which now proposed that the conference meet in Washington in September, 1921. In reply to a question he stated that he had been aided in the preparation of his resolution by Alpheus S. Snow whom, according to France, the State Department had asked to "submit special reports and advice which might be used by the peace conference during their deliberations." This was the sole expression of interest in France's lengthy reservation.[14]

Lodge then moved the adoption of the mandate reservation. Reed repeated the argument that the word mandatory was "seductive." In actual fact, he insisted, "it meant holding a people in subjection by force of arms. It is the term that has been employed in arrant hypocrisy by France and Great Britain for a century past. They have had mandatories [*sic*] and they have had protectorates in every country." He also repeated the refrain that when the mandates should have been established, American arms would have to be sent to "impose our will upon a subject people." After devoting twelve columns of the *Record* to an impassioned denunciation of the League, he reminded the Senate that Washington's birthday had just passed. Was it not, therefore, "a good time to rebaptize ourselves in the spirit of the fathers? . . . Is that not our highest duty?" Lodge called for a recorded vote on the reservation despite Hitchcock's objection. Except for a brief statement by Walsh of Montana that he thought the reservation unnecessary since he could not understand how the United States could become a mandatory

---

[13] *Congressional Record*, 66th Cong., 2nd sess., pp. 3182-3184.
[14] *Ibid.*, 66th Cong., 2nd sess., pp. 3242, 3500, 3502.

without an act of Congress, there was no other discussion of the reservation. It was approved, 68 yeas and 4 nays. The four recorded as voting against it were Jones of New Mexico, Kendrick, Walsh of Montana and Williams.[15] Walsh's reason was clear—he saw no necessity for it—but he still opposed the idea of accepting a mandate. The reasons that led Jones, Kendrick and especially Williams after Wilson's letter of January 26 can only be guessed.

This is the only reservation, with the exception of the vote to ratify on which there was any considerable change from the November results. The Democratic vote in February was almost the exact reverse of what it had been in November. At that time nine had voted in the affirmative and thirty-one in the negative. In February thirty voted for and four against. The Republican vote, however, was perfectly consistent. There had been forty-one yeas and no nays in November; in February there were thirty-eight yeas and again no nays.

Even after the decisive vote of February 21 the mandate system still had to have its innings. On March 3 Poindexter brought up again the Armenian mandate, stating that he had heard that an American army of 25,000 would be required to police Turkey. King declared that the day for temporizing about Armenia had passed—he favored an independent Armenia. Borah also had a good time denouncing the Turks. He quoted Lloyd George as having said during the war: "'As the Lord liveth, England does not want a yard of territory'." But leaving out Persia, Borah maintained, England had got at least 1,607,053 square miles of territory. In rebuttal of Borah's statement about the British acquisition of Mesopotamia Hitchcock cited article 22. He also praised the president again for his role in establishing the mandate system. Reed contended that Britain had added 3,000,000 square miles and 50,000,000 subjects. Smith of Georgia went again over the old arguments in favor of the reservation. Spencer went over each reservation, declaring that the third did "not change a single word of

[15] *Ibid.,* 66th Cong., 2nd sess., pp. 3502-3508, 3514-3515.

the existing treaty." He repeated the time-worn charge that the mandate system "would require the presence of American troops to keep order and American administrators at least to supervise the government and the imposition and the collection of taxes, and would place upon this government the responsibility for the government of people over whom we accepted such guardianship." Such a mandate might appeal to the humanitarian interests of the United States, but it would certainly be a departure from established foreign policy, he asserted. King on March 6 introduced a resolution calling upon the allied nations to compel Turkey to recognize the independence of Armenia. It was referred to the Committee on Foreign Relations. McCormick declared that the French "annexation" of Syria under the guise of a mandate had "vastly complicated" the situation in the Near East.[16]

The limited extent of America's imperialistic interests at that time is indicated by the scant interest given to former Secretary of the Treasury McAdoo's proposal to purchase Jamaica and other British possessions in the Caribbean. Kenyon regretted that no effort had been made to acquire them, but he received no support from his colleagues. Gore served notice of his intention to offer a reservation which he asked to have read and to lie on the table. In view of the assertion that the allocation of the Near Eastern mandates was dictated by considerations of oil,[17] Gore's resolution is printed in full. It provided:

> The United States understands that no mandatory power shall, without the consent of the council, enjoy any monopoly, privilege, or preference in respect of the national resources or the acquisition, development, and operation of the same in any territory placed under its control, influence, or mandate; and the United States further understands that no member of the league shall, without the consent of the council, enjoy any monopoly, privilege, or preference prejudicial to the equal rights and opportunities of any other member in respect of the natural resources or the acquisition, development, or operation of the same situate in any colony, dependency, or sphere of influence, its title or claim to which shall have been vested or confirmed by the treaty or by virtue of the action or authority of the league itself.[18]

[16] *Ibid.*, 66th Cong., 2nd sess., pp. 3793-3795, 3803-3804, 3892-3898, 3946-3947.
[17] See above, p. 4.
[18] *Congressional Record*, 66th Cong., 2nd sess., pp. 3948, 4004.

Hitchcock inserted a letter from Wilson urging support of article 10 without reservation. The proposed reservation, the president had insisted, would permit the imperialistic nations "to contnue the historic game of kings and pawns—the juggling of provinces, the old balances of power, and the inevitable wars attendant upon them." The president did not discuss the question whether article 10 guaranteed the control of these powers over their dependent areas. On March 15 (legislative day of March 11) Lodge reported the completion of the votes on the reservations brought in by the Committee on Foreign Relations.[19]

Reed found occasion on March 16 to repeat the assertion that the League would soon disappear leaving Britain in full possession of her mandated areas. Borah and Walsh of Massachusetts reiterated the charge that the Covenant had greatly increased the empires of especially Britain and France. Although the latter was probably speaking only in behalf of the Irish and the Egyptians, he propounded general questions concerning dependent areas that were not satisfactorily at the San Francisco Conference. He defied the Senate as follows:

> I now challenge . . . any Senator upon this floor to point out any section of the league covenant which gives any opportunity for subject peoples to obtain a hearing and have their claims for independence determined. I wait for an answer. [Pause.]
>
> Again I challenge any Senator to show me any provision in this league which gives an oppressed people any practical assurance of justice even if a hearing is granted, in the strange and improbable event that the oppressing nation should consent to a hearing concerning charges against itself. [Pause.]

Of course, no senator accepted the challenge. Two days later Walsh again took the floor to charge that every one who had voted for article 10 without reservation "voted to deprive subject races forever of the opportunity of outside aid and assistance." Representatives of Koreans, Egyptians, Irish, "and all other subject races" were therefore aroused, he asserted. Edge called attention to the difference between independence for Ireland which he favored and self-determination for the Virgin

[19] *Ibid.*, 66th Cong., 2nd sess., pp. 4051-4052, 4333.

Islands which the United States, he was sure, was not ready to recommend.[20]

Gore had his resolution read, explaining that it was solely designed to protect the petroleum resources of the world. Phelan found out from Lodge that it had not been before the Committee on Foreign Relations. Lodge, however, believed, that the United States was fully protected by the mandate reservation. Phelan, however, pointed out that if Congress should accept a mandate, the resources would come within the control of Congress, but that Gore's resolution applied entirely to mandates held by other countries. Since the League was dealing as an organized entity in mandates and since the United States would not be present, could the United States interpose a veto?[21] Lodge replied that all he knew was that the conquered territories had been divided long ago.[22] Phelan insisted that the resolution should prevail—he evidently understood better than did Lodge what Gore was driving at. On a division, however, the resolution was rejected. Except the fifteenth reservation (Irish self-determination), which had to be reserved for a separate vote, the ayes favored approval in the Committee of the Whole of the other reservations.[23]

On the crucial day, March 19, the Senate took its final vote on ratification. Lenroot analyzed each article of the Covenant and showed how it was affected by the reservations. With respect to article 22 he queried:

> In voting to reject this treaty do the Senators who are following the President take the position that they are against the treaty because they want the President of the United States to accept a mandate for Armenia, or a mandate for any other country, without the consent of Congress?
>
> Who among you will be foolhardy enough to take that position before the American people?

Walsh of Montana admitted that the Democratic senators found themselves faced with two embarrassing choices: "They

[20] *Ibid.*, 66th Cong., 2nd sess., pp. 4384, 4393-4396, 4514.

[21] After prolonged negotiations an agreement was reached by which American interests were permitted to acquire twenty-five per cent of the shares of the Turkish Petroleum Company.—Edward M. Earle, "The Turkish Petroleum Company, a Study in Oleaginous Diplomacy," *Political Science Quarterly*, XXXIX (June, 1924), 265-279.

[22] See above, p. 4.

[23] *Congressional Record*, 66th Cong., 2nd sess., pp. 4522-4523.

may vote to reject the treaty, at least for the present, or they may vote to ratify it with reservations that emasculate, if they do not destroy, features of the covenant that, in their judgment, are in no small degree essential to insure its successful operation as a means of averting war." Hoke Smith again devoted a column to repeating his charge about Smuts's handiwork, the need for a billion dollars a year and 250,000 American boys to police some foreign country at the behest of a presidential agent in Switzerland. He also condemned the I. L. O. Owen did not doubt that the principles of article 22 would "develop into complete liberty for all the subjejct nations [he was discussing primarily Ireland and Egypt, the latter of which was his special interest] in the world as rapidly as they can be taught to stand by themselves under the strenuous conditions of the modern world." Indeed, he seemed to think that the principles were *not* applicable to the mandated areas, for he made clear that "when we speak of the right of self-determination, we do not speak of uninformed savages to organize a modern democracy. They have no capacity."[24]

These were the last words spoken on the mandate system during this memorable debate. On the final roll call the resolution of ratification with reservations showed 49 yeas and 35 nays. Twenty-one Democrats and twenty-eight Republicans voted in the affirmative as against four Democrats and thirty-five Republicans in November. Twenty-three Democrats and twelve Republicans cast their votes in the negative as against forty-two Democrats and thirteen Republicans in November.[25]

---

[24]*Ibid.*, 66th Cong., 2nd sess., pp. 4575-4577, 4590, 4595

[25]*Ibid.*, 66th Cong., 2nd sess., pp. 4599-4600.

CHAPTER VI

THE FINAL ACT: REJECTION OF THE ARMENIAN MANDATE

Even after the Senate had voted decisively against the Treaty of Versailles with reservations, interest in Armenia persisted. On May 13 a resolution introduced by Harding congratulating Armenia upon the recognition of her independence, expressing sympathy for her and authorizing the president to send ships and marines to protect American life and property in Batum and Baku was agreed to. Shortly thereafter, May 24, Wilson sent a letter to Congress expressing his gratification that the San Remo Conference had just formally resolved to address an appeal to the United States government asking that it accept a mandate for Armenia. He "urgently" advised and requested that Congress grant the executive the power, for he earnestly believed that the people of the United States wished that it be done. "The sympathy for Armenia among our people," he continued, "has sprung from untainted consciences, pure Christian faith, and an earnest desire to see Christian people everywhere succored in their time of suffering, and lifted from their abject subjection and distress and enabled to stand upon their own feet and take their place among the free nations of the world." But on May 27 Lodge reported a concurrent resolution from the Committee on Foreign Relations respectfully declining the president's request.[1]

When the resolution was debated two days later, Hitchcock himself declared that he did not favor granting the president's request, but that he was afraid that the resolution would discourage the Armenians and encourage their enemies. He therefore submitted an amendment providing for the appointment by the president of three Americans to act with a like number of Armenians under a chairman selected by the six. This joint commission would offer for sale in the United States bonds for

[1] *Congressional Record,* 66th Cong., 2nd sess., pp. 6978-6979, 7533-7534, 7714.

the Armenian government not exceeding $50,000,000 to help in the economic rehabilitation of the country. Lodge expressed his deepest sympathy for the Armenians, but declared his complete opposition to keeping an army of 60,000 troops in Armenia for an indefinite time and to becoming involved in an expenditure estimated by the Harbord Report to be $275,000,000 for the first year.[2] Williams supported the president's request because, he believed, the presence of the Aremican uniform would suffice to restore order and the American people would want to make this contribution to world peace.

Jones of New Mexico interjected the most important point—he asserted that acceptance of the mandate was totally aside from the question of membership in the League. But, it seemed to him, Armenia was in the class of mandates that could " 'be provisionally recognized subject to the rendering of administrative advice and assistance by a Mandatory until such time as they are able to stand alone.' " The Hitchcock amendment would provide that kind of assistance. But Lenroot insisted that the limited assistance would leave the Armenians worse off than they had been before since it would shut out acceptance of the mandate by any other nation. Jones retorted that other nations could share in the type of assistance suggested by Hitchcock.

Smith of Georgia demanded what authority existed for the United States to engage in "altruistic" undertakings. Lodge pointed out the vagueness of the Armenian boundaries. Smith added that the new republic would be used as a buffer against Soviet Russia. An army of at least 100,000 would be required; a mandate over Armenia would be much more complicated and dangerous than the "mandatory" which the United States had recently attempted to exercise over Mexico. The Armenian mandate was, moreover, an illustration of the burden the United States would have assumed if she had ratified the Covenant without "nullifying" reservations. Thomas suggested that if the United States accepted the Armenian mandate, she could

---

[2]The Report, dated October 16, 1919, is in *ibid.*, 66th Cong., 2nd sess., pp. 7877-7886.

hardly refuse others. Smith agreed with him. Thomas then asked Smith if it would be better for the United States to assume a mandate over Mexico. But Smith replied: "The objection to a mandate over Mexico is that it is so near home it might contribute to the welfare of our own people." He did not explain this cryptic remark. Brandegee later in the day pointed out the president's failure to indicate the exact nature of the responsibilities the United States would have to assume. Like Smith he believed that no constitutional authority existed for the United States "to promote philanthropic projects or to uplift the Armenian or any other European or Asiatic or African peoples." He was willing, however, for the Senate to express sympathy for the Armenians and to consider whether a private loan might be raised for the purposes indicated by Hitchcock. France was allowed to have printed again his resolution of February 26 authorizing the president to assemble a conference in September, 1921. He then gave a long discourse in which he alleged: "This so-called League of Nations would attempt to chain the newly liberated spirit of mankind to the imperial chariot of the old order and drag it in humiliation into slavery and despair."[3]

During the debate, May 31, on Hitchcock's amendment Reed made his usual speech about imposing upon the United States "the guardianship of the world." Walsh of Montana contended that there was nothing in article 22 that required the mandatory to provide military protection. At all events, the United States could accept the mandate subject to the understanding that it would not have to render any military aid toward the preservation of the integrity of Armenia. Reed rejoined that the president's comments, as reported in the press, and the Harbord Report showed that such aid would be necessary. When Walsh made the suggestion that other nations could share with the United States in furnishing military aid, Norris made the pointed observation that "it would naturally and logically follow that in every other mandate anywhere else on the face of

[3] *Ibid.*, 66th Cong., 2nd sess., pp. 7875-7890, 7914-7920.

the earth the United States would be expected to furnish some of the soldiers." Walsh had to admit that the United States could decline to do so. Reed triumphantly pointed out that other nations could do so likewise if the United States accepted the Armenian mandate. He painted an alarming picture of Armenia surrounded by "250,000,000" Mohammedans, on the verge of revolt against imperialistic powers, and by Russia. If the United States had to accept a mandate, let it be over Japan —"let us have a religious war between Japan and the United States." There was much that needed to be done at home. Consequently, "Back to the doctrine of nationalism, of Americanism, to the cultivation of friendly relations with all countries and entanglements with none."[4]

On June 1, the final day of debate, Thomas gave the familiar reasons for not accepting a mandate. Robinson asked for rejection of the Lodge resolution or modification that would permit the United States either by herself or in conjunction with her allies to aid Armenia. He argued that the United States should openly aid Armenia through a mandate rather than seek to govern it by the clandestine manner of sending troops to protect American life and property. He supported a substitute drafted by King which would empower the president to enter into arrangements to cooperate with the Council or members of the League "for the proper protection of Armenia, including the advancement of supplies and commodities essential for the health and life of its people and the preservation of its political independence and territorial integrity." Unless the United States supported Armenia, "Christianity on its eastern frontier will receive a staggering blow and the Crescent there will be uplifted above the Cross." But Brandegee called Armenia "the plague spot of Europe, Asia, Africa." He believed that the treasurer of the United States could be enjoined from spending money for the purpose of protecting the Armenians from the Turks. He ridiculed the idea of becoming a mandatory under a League of which the United States was not a member and

[4] *Ibid.*, 66th Cong., 2nd sess., pp. 7960-7970.

submitting an annual report to this League. "Could international madness proceed further than that?" the Republican irreconcilable inquired. What would be the fate of an amendment to the Constitution giving Congress power to levy taxes to help people in Asia?

Walsh of Montana pointed out that the United States was spending money in Haiti although the United States did not possess sovereignty over it. Brandegee in an effort to dispose of the question as quickly as possible offered an amendment granting the president the power he requested. McCormick reviewed the history of the "unspeakable Turk" and plowed not only in Armenia but in Asia and Africa "the furrow which will be sown with salt and fertilized in the blood of our young men." Lenroot discussed the military forces that would be required in case of war with Russia. Lodge opposed sending troops and spending money for an indefinite period; he doubted the constitutionality of the proposed mandate despite his sympathy for the Armenians. Pomerene and Walsh desired additional information about the responsibilities that would devolve upon the United States. The latter contended that "it is clearly contemplated in the covenant that a mandate over ignorant, black savages of South Africa shall be something essentially different from a mandate, for instance, over Poland or a mandate over Armenia." He repeated his statement that the United States exercised in substance a mandate over Haiti and added Panama. Underwood felt that the question should not be decided until the United States had decided upon the way of making peace with Germany. If the United States accepted the mandate as a member of the League, she would have a voice in the administration of Armenia. If not, she would be "under the power of the governing board of other nations in whose councils we have no part." McCumber was utterly opposed to acceptance since the United States had not entered the League.

Hitchcock moved to have the report recommitted for further study. Williams reluctantly opposed because, he alleged, the Committee would keep it there until the next session. Recommitment was defeated, 34 yeas to 43 nays, on an almost strict party vote. Brandegee's amendment was defeated 12 yeas (all Democrats) to 62. Hitchcock's amendment was rejected, 34 yeas to 41 nays, and the Lodge resolution was agreed to, 52 yeas, 23 nays. All negative votes were cast by Democrats. Ten Democrats deserted Wilson to vote with Lodge against the acceptance of the Armenian mandate. They were Beckham, Dial (South Carolina), Gerry, Harris, Nugent, Pomerene, Reed, Smith of Georgia, Thomas, and Walsh of Massachusetts.[5]

These ten votes would still have been insufficient to give the president the power that he requested. Not even the appeal to save the Cross from the Crescent could overcome the isolationist, personal, constitutional and financial objections coupled with the desire to keep the "boys" at home. The United States had gone to war to make the world safe for democracy, but having suffered some 348,000 casualties and spent $35,000,000,000 the American people were eager to return to their own problems and let the rest of the world shuffle along as best it could. The American people were neither imperialistic nor altruistic in 1919 and 1920. This second world war has made them conscious of the 1,700 miles from Dakar on the West Coast of Africa to Natal in Brazil and of the vital strategic importance of the South Pacific islands. They are therefore desirous of acquiring the outlying posts that will protect them from invasion, but there is no evidence of any greater altruism in 1945 than there was in 1919 or 1920.

---

[5] *Ibid.*, 66th Cong., 2nd sess., pp. 8051-8073.

APPENDIX

The following articles of the Covenant of the League of Nations, as ratified, are quoted for convenient reference:

3. . . . At meetings of the Assembly each Member of the League shall have one vote and may not have more than three Representatives.

4. . . . The Council may deal at its meetings with any matter within the sphere of action of the League or affecting the peace of the world.

10. The Members of the League undertake to respect and preserve as against external aggression the territorial integrity and existing political independence of all Members of the League. In case of any such aggression or in case of any threat or danger of such aggression, the Council shall advise upon the means by which this obligation shall be fulfilled.

11. Any war or threat of war, whether immediately affecting any of the Members of the League or not, is hereby declared a matter of concern to the whole League, and the League shall take any action that may be deemed wise and effectual to safeguard the peace of nations. In case any such emergency should arise, the Secretary-General shall, on the request of any Member of the League, forthwith summon a meeting of the Council.

It is also declared to be the friendly right of each Member of the League to bring to the attention of the Assembly or of the Council any circumstance whatever affecting international relations which threatens to disturb international peace or the good understanding between nations upon which peace depends.

21. Nothing in this Covenant shall be deemed to affect the validity of international engagements, such as treaties of arbitration or regional understandings like the Monroe Doctrine, for securing the maintenance of peace.

22. To those colonies and territories which as a consequence of the late war have ceased to be under the sovereignty of the States which formerly governed them and which are inhabited by peoples not yet able to stand by themselves under the strenuous conditions of the modern world, there should be applied the principle that the well-being and development of such peoples form a sacred trust of civilization and that securities for the performance of this trust should be embodied in this Covenant.

The best method of giving practical effect to this principle is that the tutelage of such peoples should be entrusted to advanced nations who, by reason of their resources, their experience or their geographical position can best undertake this responsibility, and who are willing to accept it, and that this tutelage should be exercised by them as Mandatories on behalf of the League.

The character of the mandate must differ according to the stage of the development of the people, the geographical situation of the territory, its economic conditions, and other similar circumstances.

Certain communities formerly belonging to the Turkish Empire have reached a stage of development where their existence as independent nations can be provisionally recognized subject to the rendering of administrative advice and assistance by a Mandatory until such time as they are able to stand alone. The wishes of these communities must be a principal consideration in the selection of the Mandatory.

Other peoples, especially those of Central Africa, are at such a stage that the Mandatory must be responsible for the administration of the territory under conditions which will guarantee freedom of conscience and religion, subject only to the maintenance of public order and morals, the prohibition of abuses such as the slave trade, the arms traffic, and the liquor traffic, and the prevention of the establishment of fortifications or military and naval bases and of military training of the natives for other than police purposes and the defense of the territory, and will also secure equal opportunities for the trade and commerce of other Members of the League.

There are territories, such as Southwest Africa and certain of the South Pacific Islands, which, owing to their sparseness of their population, or their small size, or their remoteness from the centers of civilization, or their geographical contiguity to the territory of the Mandatory, and other circumstances, can be best administered under the laws of the Mandatory as integral portions of its territory, subject to the safeguards above mentioned in the interests of the indigenous population.

In every case of mandate, the Mandatory shall render to the Council an annual report in reference to the territory committed to its charge.

The degree of authority, control, or administration to be exercised by the Mandatory shall, if not previously agreed upon by the Members of the League, be explicitly defined in each case by the Council.

A permanent Commission shall be constituted to receive and examine the annual reports of the Mandatories and to advise the Council on all matters relating to the observance of the mandates.

23. Subject to and in accordance with the provisions of international conventions existing or hereafter to be agreed upon, the Members of the League: (a) will endeavor to secure and maintain fair and humane conditions of labor for men, women, and children, both in their own countries and in all countries to which their commercial and industrial relations extend, and for that purpose will establish and maintain the necessary international organizations; (b) undertake to secure just treatment of the native inhabitants of territories under their control; (c) will entrust the League with the general supervision over the execution of agreements with regard to the traffic in women and children, and the traffic in opium and other dangerous drugs; (d) will entrust the League with the general supervision of the trade in arms and ammunition with the countries in which the control of this traffic is necessary in the common interest; (e) will make provision to secure and maintain freedom of communications and of transit and of equitable treatment for the commerce of all Members of the League. In this connection, the special necessities of the regions devastated during the war of 1914-1918 shall be borne in mind; (f) will endeavor to take steps in matters of international concern for the prevention and control of disease.

BIBLIOGRAPHY

The principal source is naturally the *Congressional Record*, 64th Congress, 2nd session, 65th Congress, 1st, 2nd and 3rd sessions; 66th Congress, 1st and 2nd sessions; and the Hearings before the Senate Committee on Foreign Relations, Senate Document 106, 66th Congress, 1st session.

Henry Cabot Lodge is the only senator who has given a full account of the debates. But his *The Senate and the League of Nations* (New York, 1925) adds nothing of value for this study. Karl Schriftgiesser's *The Gentleman from Massachusetts: Henry Cabot Lodge* (Boston, 1944) gives no new evidence and does not even list in the index the word "mandate."

The two principal secondary sources, totally inadequate for the debates on the mandates but indispensable for the rejection of the treaty, are Denna F. Fleming, *The United States and the League of Nations* (New York, 1932) and Chapter X of W. Stull Holt's *Treaties Defeated by the Senate.*

The *Biographical Directory of the American Congress, 1774-1927* (House Document 783, 69th Congress, 2nd session, Washington, 1928) contains brief sketches as well as the political affiliation of senators.

James W. Gerard, former American ambassador to Germany, and others wrote a series of articles, published by the Armenian National Union of New York, 1919 [?], urging the acceptance of the Armenian mandate.

Quincy Wright's *Mandates under the League of Nations* (Chicago, 1930) is the best general book on the mandate system as a whole, but of insignificant value for the Senate debates.

The writer's *Operation of the Mandate System in Africa, with an Introduction on the Problem of the Mandates in the Post-War World* (Washington, 1942) similarly is without value for the Senate debates.

Thomas A. Bailey's *Woodrow Wilson and the Great Betrayal* (New York, 1945), which appeared after this book had gone to press, has only very brief references to the Senate debates on the mandate systm.

INDEX